Rich Man in Training
VII Pillars
To Obtain Your True Riches

Thomas J. Slaughter

TRU Statement Inc.

Copyright © 2017 by Thomas J. Slaughter. All rights reserved. This book or any portion thereof may not be reproduced or used in any manner whatsoever without the express written permission of the publisher except for the use of brief quotations in a book review or scholarly journal. For information email info@richmanintraining.com

TRU Statement Inc. books may be purchased for educational, business, or sales promotional use. Special discounts are available on quantity purchases by corporations, associations, educators, and others. For details, contact Special Markets Department: Tel: (866) 246-5838 or email spmarkets@richmanintraining.com

For speaking engagements and presentations please contact TRU Statement Inc. engagement team: Tel. (866) 246-5838 or email engagement@richmanintraining.com

U.S. trade bookstores and wholesalers: Please contact TRU Statement Inc Tel: (866) 246-5838 or email tbw@richmanintraining.com

First Printing: 2017

ISBN-13: 978-1948085007
ISBN-10: 1948085003
www.richmanintraining.com

Dedication

Rich Man in Training is decicated to those who wish to obtain their *True Riches*. I wish for you to become a True Rich Man or Woman and to share your Riches with the world.

Contents

Dedication	iii
Preface	vii
Introduction	1
Pillar I – Know Thy Riches	5
Pillar II - Faith is not an Option!	23
Pillar III – What's Your Time Worth?	35
Pillar IV – Live Intentional	57
Pillar V - Working Knowledge	69
Pillar VI - The Cohorts	85
Pillar VII – Resourceful Fear	107
In Conclusion	119
BIOs	121
FREE RESOURCES	127

Preface

In August 2002 I was inmate T11199, who had been sitting in the hole for the past two months, as the result of being a participant in a 300-man prison riot. I had been stabbed multiple times in this riot, and now laid alone in a prison cell taking inventory on my life. As my physical wounds healed and my psychological wounds worsened, every thought drove me into a deeper state of depression as they tormented me with every passing minute; finally, my mind broke, and suicide became my favorite thought. I laid there for hours with tears rolling down my eyes, contemplating the best way to end my life. It was fair to say I hit rock bottom as I questioned my very existence in this world.

So there I laid on my bunk, a 21-year-old high school dropout and convicted drug dealer, who wanted to quit life. Little did I know at that time, I would one day become a college graduate with a wonderful career; enjoying luncheons with politicians; advisor to corporate executives; lecturer to university students; speaking to the masses; raise a beautiful family with my wonderful wife; and not want for anything financially.

If you told me then how prosperous I would be today, I would not have believed you – how could I? My wife was sleeping on the floor of her friend's apartment, scared with our one-year daughter in her arms; meanwhile, I was inmate T11199, serving a six-year prison sentence, contemplating ending my life. The best I could have hoped for, was to stay alive long enough to be released from prison, hopefully not get murdered before my release, or go back to prison after I got released.

So, you might be wondering, "What had changed in my life, that took me from a prison cell to a life full of my *Riches*?" Throughout the past 14 years, and by the grace of God, I've been blessed to become a student of *Rich Men* and *Rich Women,* of all walks of life – making me a **Rich Man in Training**.

I took the knowledge they bestowed upon me, applied it to my own life, and have watched it flourish. One by one, I began to obtain my *True Riches* in family, relationships, finances, community, career, and education.

Regardless of my background and doubts from others, on my ability to succeed, I've continue to excel and obtain my *True Riches*. It is now my burning desire, to share the knowledge that was given to me, which transformed my life, and has taking me from *Ruins to Riches*.

My intentions for writing this book is to inspire you to obtain the *Riches* you seek; knowing that it can and will be done. I pray God blesses you with all the *Riches* of your heart's desire, and through the knowledge I'm passing to you, from the rich men and women I learned from, you shall succeed.

God bless you,

Thomas J. Slaughter
Claremont, CA
September 26, 2017

"You can't have True Riches, until you understand what constitutes True Riches!"

Thomas J. Slaughter –

Introduction

The very concept of **Rich Man in Training** began as a thought in 2012, while I was speaking at a conference in Corona, California. I was sharing my life experience as a story of inspiration, to a group of young men and women who suffered from a life of defeats, personal tragedies, failures, and doubts. These young men and women were victims of years of abuse, convicted of crimes, suffered the loss of a loved one, battled with drug addiction, went through a divorce, or had some other challenges in their life that left them broken in spirit, hope, and vision. I could relate to them all, as I, too, once was broken in spirit, hope, and vision.

As I continued to share my life experiences, I frequently used the term *True Riches*, to define what matter most to me. After sharing my experience with the audience, a young man asked me, "How do you know what your *True Riches* are?"

At that moment, I realized it was not clear what constituted *True Riches*, or how one was to obtain them. Everything I shared up to that point, was an idea or concept. However, where was the blueprint to determine and obtain one's riches. I did my best to refer them to books that helped mold me; however, the books I referred them to, were also conceptual and lacked practical use. Those books commonly focused in one area of riches such as spirituality or finance. These resources failed to provide a comprehensive guide on defining and pursuing *True Riches,* which is what **Rich Man in Training** is designed to do.

Rich Man in Training provides a practical guide to identify and obtain your *True Riches*, using 7 vital principles, which I call the **7 Pillars**. Each pillar will help you build your blueprint on obtaining your *True Riches*, just as it has guided me in building my blueprint.

These pillars were taught to me by spiritual teachers, business executives, scholars, philosophers, philanthropist, and by divine knowledge that was bestowed upon me over my 36 years. It's these same pillars, that helped me break away from suicidal thoughts in a prison cell, to living a life full of *Riches*.

This book was not written as *just* a "How to Guide". It was written as a resource to help you obtain the riches in life you could only imagine. Through realistic information and knowledge, you can begin to use it immediately. You will have the opportunity to download the resources shared in this book, from the **"*Rich Man in Training* Free Resources"** page at **richmanintraining.com**.

What's a *Rich Man in Training*?

1. A person who is looking to enrich their life and the lives of others.

2. One who is determined to find success and happiness in all areas of their life.

3. Any person seeking to elevate their life and obtain their *True Riches*.

Pillar I – Know Thy Riches

"All achievements, all earned Riches, have their beginning in an idea."

Napoleon Hill –

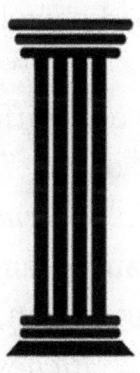

The very foundation and **First Pillar** of all rich men and women is knowing what their *True Riches* are – **Know thy Riches.** When I speak of *Riches*, I'm not speaking of your income; I'm not speaking of personal finances; I'm not speaking of accumulated assets; I'm not speaking of money at all. I'm speaking of what you value most in life. What you hold nearest and dearest to your heart. It's your reason as to "Why?" It's the first cause of everything you do. It's your purpose in life. Think of it as your personal currency, and the result of you obtaining it, results in finances, love, stability, security, and abundance of success in all aspects of your life.

Everyone will have a different definition of *True Riches*. A Buddhist may define *True Riches* as enlightenment, community, and virtue. *True Riches* in the heart of a Christian, may be God, family, and goodwill. An Entrepreneur may acknowledge innovation, or helping mankind with a new technology, as *True Riches*. As for a Scholar, *True Riches* may be a new research, discovery, or concept.

Until you clearly define what your *True Riches* are, you will never obtain them. You'll never find the success and satisfaction in life that a *true* rich man enjoys. You'll always be looking for something to fulfill you; living life as an empty vessel, full of doubts, disappointments, and self-regrets – I know, I've been there. I lived like this for so many years, sabotaging my own life, because I had not identified my *True Riches*.

This chapter is going to help you define your *True Riches*, and build a roadmap to obtain them.

What's your Riches?

Regardless of what your circumstances are today, good or bad, you must have a clear defined image of what you constitute as riches. **Know thy Riches!** If you were to ask a rich man or woman to define their riches, they could tell you exactly what they are, without a second thought. It's their compass in life; It's how they measure their success; It's how they set their goals in life. What one person considers as riches, may not be another person's thought or definition. If you ask Bill Gates or Jay-Z how they define *True Riches*, I'm confident it would significantly differ from yours or mine. Everyone has a unique list of personal riches. The question is, "What is yours!"

*"Poverty is anomaly to rich people;
it is very difficult to make out why people who want dinner
do not ring the bell."*

Walter Bagehot –

Know Thy Riches

Defining your Riches

The quote by Walter Bagehot, resonated with me for some time. "Why people who want dinner do not ring the bell." What I concluded was people do not know what they want for dinner. They know they are hungry, but they do not know exactly what they want to eat. A good example of this is to think of a drive thru at a fast food restaurant. You and your friends pull up to the intercom system to place your order. Then someone in the car says to the driver, "Hold on, let me see what's on the menu." Although that person has been to that restaurant over a hundred times, they always have the tendency to say, "Hold on, let me see what's on the menu." After minutes of debating the menu options, they are ready to order.

Now let's think about this for minute. They had all the opportunity to think about what they wanted to order, while they were on the way to the restaurant. In today's world, they could have looked up the menu on their smart phone. They could have asked someone, "What's good on the menu?" While waiting in line at the fast food drive through, they could have looked ahead at the menu. However, they waited until they got to the intercom and then decided, "Let me see what's on the menu."

Think of the time wasted by not knowing what they wanted. Every time they go to the drive-thru window, they debate for minutes. Over time, these minutes add up to hours. More importantly, they do not ring the dinner bell, because they truly do not know what they want. They waited until someone else asked them, "What do you want?" If you live a life waiting for someone to ask you what you want, then you'll never obtain your *True Riches*.

So, let's do our first exercise. I want you to define your *True Riches*. What do you want must out of life? This is how you are going to ring the bell to get your dinner!

Take out a piece of paper and write down all your personal desires. Is it finances, career, family, spirituality, love, friendship. I want you to be open and honest with yourself, and be specific. It's no shame in being specific and knowing exactly what you want. The only shame in not being specific and not ringing the bell, because you don't know what you want. Be clear!

For example: I want a new White 2016 Maserati Gran Turismo S, with carbon interior package, and tooled MC aluminum pedals.

Note: Do not write down what you feel society thinks; what your parents think you ought to think; what you think someone else believes you ought to think. It's your heart's desires.

After you complete your list, I want you to look at it carefully and ask yourself this question, "Why do I desire these items?" Is it family, status, love, power, spirituality, shelter, security, or whatever other ideas you may have. Once you determine why you want what you heart desires. I want you to write it down.

For examples:

    1. *Family*
    2. *Security*
    3. *Finances*
    4. *Spirituality*
    5. *Relationships*
    6. *Family Legacy*
    7. *Charity*
    8. *Community*

These are your *True Riches*!

"What you get by achieving your goals is not as important as what you become by achieving your goals."

Zig Ziglar –

Goals to Riches

Now that you have created your list of *True Riches*, everything you do in life, from this point forward, must be focused on obtaining them.

Your every thought must be toward your riches. Your every action must be toward your riches. Every relationship you build going forward must be built in alignment with you obtaining your riches. These are now your pillars; Your purpose; Your goals; Anything contrary to it, threatens your success, and will only keep you from obtaining your *True Riches*.

My First List of Riches

On November 19th, 2003, around 2am, I wrote my first set of goals based on my list of riches, which I had created a few weeks prior. At that time, I was at the lowest point in my life. I was serving a 6-year prison sentence; I did not know where my daughter and girlfriend were; I had not spoken with my family for months; I stayed drunk on prison made wine (pruno), and high from marijuana smoke to cope with my situation; I harbored a relentless hate in my heart, but most importantly, I felt no purpose – no real reason to live.

However, this all changed when another inmate asked me, "What's the most important thing to you in life?"

I couldn't answer his question. So, I responded to him the best I could by saying, "Does it really matter, look where we are at?"

He told me he had the same answer 10 years ago, when he was five years into his life sentence. At that moment, he challenged me to write down everything that mattered to me, and show him the list when I was finished. Well, I didn't have much else to do, so I took him up on the challenge.

Without much thought, I wrote out my list. It started with money, houses, cars, etc. When I finished my list, I did as he asked and showed him my list. He studied my list for a few minutes. Then he asked me, "Why is money, houses, and cars so important to you."

I told him, "It's for my family. I want them to have the best of everything. They deserve the best of everything."

He, then asked me, "How often did you think about your family while you made your list?"

I told him, "Just about everything on my list was for my family."

He then asked me, "Why isn't your family on the list?" This is when I had a *come to Jesus moment*. He opened my eyes to see the first of my *True Riches*. He went on to explain that he noticed everything on my list was driven by me wanting to do something better for my family. So, he asked me to think about this and create a new list.

Over the course of the next couple of days, I worked on my new list, which was one of the hardest things I ever had to do. Contemplating my new list, I had to face reality as my *come to Jesus moments* continued. I had to admit to myself how wrong I had been. After days of soul searching, I finally created my first list of riches. It was a simple three item list; however, this list was the start of me becoming a *Rich Man in Training*!

Thomas' List from 2003 - 2008

1. My families love
2. Be a pillar for my family and community
3. Take care of my family

Based on my 2003 list of personal riches, I could clearly define my goals and measure my personal levels of success. Each of my goals was based on me obtaining my *True Riches*. If I had a goal that did not help me obtain my *True Riches*, I simply changed it. I always had to ask myself, "What would it take to obtain my riches?" With my new perspective, I wrote down my goals, under each of my riches, as seen on the next page.

1. **My families love**
    a. Marry my girlfriend
    b. Take my daughter to her first day of 1st grade
    c. Let my family know how much I love them

2. **Be a pillar for my family and community**
    a. Get a better education
    b. Transfer knowledge to the youth
    c. Be an inspiration to others

3. **Take care of my family**
    a. Buy a house
    b. Financially support my family
    c. Start my own business

This began to give me a clear picture on what I needed to pursue my riches. However, I needed to create a blueprint on how I was going to accomplish my goals. This came in the form of creating tasks.

For each goal set, I list specific tasks that I need to complete, to reach my goal. I knew each task had to be *SMART*. Specific, Measurable, Attainable, Relevant, and Time Bound; something that I learned reading an old project management book in the prison library. Therefore, every goal I set included a list of tasks.

I created the following task list for my goal of getting a better education:

- o Complete my Bachelor's Degree by 2010

- o Learn something new each week that will help me improve in: finances, family, health, spirituality, and career.

During the time of defining my goals and tasks, I did not truly know to what depth of success I was going to have. I was happy with the idea, that I now had a blueprint. This blueprint gave me hope and desire. It gave me something that I could strive for, because I now had a clear picture of what I wanted out of life.

When I started to reach my goals, I got better at defining my tasks and became more focused on my personal riches. Everything I accomplished was the result of me defining what constituted my *True Riches*, and finding a way to obtain them.

To put things into perspective, I want to show you how my first list of Riches transformed my life, from year 2001 to 2010:

- In 2001, at the age of 20, I was sentenced to six years in prison for possession of cocaine based substance (crack) for intent to sale and possession of a firearm.

- In 2002, I was stabbed multiple times in a riot; then placed in Administrative Segregation (The Hole) for several months, until I was transferred from a Southern California prison (a couple of hours from my home), to a Northern California prison (too far for family to travel on a regular basis). In short, I was completely isolated from my family. I had lost all hope, and my heart darkened with a hate so deep, life had no meaning to me. I would have rather been dead; many nights I wished someone would end my life. Violence had become my release and self-expression during this time.

- In 2003, my personal enlightenment began. I developed ideas through reading books in religion, Greek philosophy, critical thinking, and business strategy. I listened to older inmates, with life sentences, explain what they would do if they had the opportunity at freedom. Then new ideas began to take shape as I listed my riches and defined my goals. I started to disassociate myself from all that would interfere with me obtaining my *True Riches*. I disassociated myself from my gang, which was not an easy thing to do. I disassociated myself from all my street associates, and stopped drinking and smoking dope. I needed a clear mind to move forward.

- In 2005, I was released from prison. I enrolled into Community College, obtained employment as a warehouse worker, and had the first opportunity to spend a holiday with my family in over 5 years.

- In 2006, I got married to the mother of my daughter, secured a permanent position as a corporate analyst, using the skills I obtained in my computer programming class at the community college, and purchased my first home with my beautiful wife.

- In 2007, I transferred to the local university as a business major, started volunteering as a mentor for at-risk youth, and was elected as the advisory board president of a local non-profit.

- In 2009, my wife and I bought our second home, built our income into the six-figure range, and started to live the life we had wished for, since we were 17 years old.

- In 2010, I was promoted to a middle management position, for the corporation I began working for, in 2006, graduated college with Bachelor's degree in business administration, and started a small business with my wife.

The Result of Knowing my Riches

In the summer of 2010 my wife and I were sitting on a balcony overlooking the vineyards of a winery in Temecula, California; at that moment, she told me how proud she was of me. This was one of the greatest moments in my life. I realized I made it against all odds. I obtained the riches I had previously written, while in that cold prison cell.

I was no rap star, professional athlete, lawyer, doctor, banker, or some other professional. I was a convicted drug dealer with no education; a teen father with a broken spirit and no vision. However, because I defined my riches, I defied logic. The reason I can say I defied logic, is because statically, I was not supposed to be sitting at a winery with my wife, discussing our steps on how to obtain our next level of riches, now that we had exceeded our previous level of riches.

Statically, I was supposed to be back in prison, instead of the accomplished young man I had become. Furthermore, I had not *just* become accomplished, I was excelling at a rate that pushed passed many of my peers, who did not have the setbacks and challenges I had. I was not just surviving, I excelled at life and enriched all those around me, but I did nothing special. Rich men and women have been doing this for years. They could clearly define their riches, understand their personal currency, set their goals, and define the tasks necessary to obtain their *True Riches*. I simply followed their system. The system that I'm now sharing with you.

Creating your Goals and Tasks

As a final exercise to this chapter, I would like you to create your goals and set your tasks to obtain your riches.

Start by listing your *"True Riches"*. Next, under each of your *"True Riches"*, write the "Goals" you must accomplish to obtain your *"True Riches."* Then under your *"Goals"*, list the *"Tasks"* that you must complete to reach your *"Goals."* Below is an example on how you can do this exercise.

Remember, your *"Goals"* and *"Tasks"* must be SMART. Specific, Measurable, Relevant, and Time Bound. To complete this exercise. You can download the Rich Man in Training **"Riches, Goals, and Tasks Planner"** from **richmanintraining.com** resources page.

Example:

Riches – Be a pillar for my family and community
- **Goal** – Get a better education
  - **Task** – Complete my Bachelor's Degree by 2010
  - Learn something new each week that will help me improve in: finances, family, health, spirituality, and career.

Transgressions of Riches

The last thing I would like to address in this chapter, is to watch that your riches do not transgress upon the natural laws of life. What I mean by this, is that your riches should not harm society, individuals, or yourself. If it conflicts with the natural laws of life, by default it will end badly. I cannot stress this enough. The Bible has a well-known passage in 1 Timothy 6:10 KJV, that explains this pitfall very well.

"For the love of money is the root of all evil: which while some coveted after, they have erred from the Faith, and pierced themselves through with many sorrows."

I'm not saying the money is evil. What I'm showing you is the root of what you desire, should not error. If the root to your riches brings harm to you or others, it will bring you sorrow. If your riches transgress the natural laws of life, it will bring you sorrow.

We've seen this too many times. Drug dealers like Rick Ross, who amass a large amount of money, to turn around and lose it all and go to prison. CEO's like Kenneth Lay of Enron, who collapsed an entire corporation do to their personal riches, conflicting with natural laws of life.

A perfect example of this transgression, is in the case of Bernard "Bernie" Madoff. He was one of the most well-respected stock brokers, investment advisers, and financiers on Wall Street. He was a chairman of the NASDAQ stock market. We would like to believe his personal riches would have enriched others. He defrauded his closest friends, clients, and thousands of people by stealing billions from them in a Ponzi scheme. Through his transgressions, he was sentenced to 150 years in prison and forfeiture $17 billion. However, this was the least of the penalties of his transgressions. His transgressions left his family, and others, in absolute ruins. His brother-in-law was sentenced to prison, his son committed suicide, and several of his clients lost millions. What he did was not just criminal, it was a clear transgression against the natural laws of life. His family name will forever bare the shame of his actions.

Keystones of the Pillar

1. The very foundation of a rich man is *Knowing thy Riches*.

2. Only when one knows thy riches, can they build goals to obtain them.

3. Maintain continuous progress through SMART (Specific, Measurable, Attainable, Relevant) tasks.

4. The riches you seek should not transgress the natural laws of life.

Pillar II - Faith is not an Option!

"To one who has Faith, no explanation is necessary. To one without Faith, no explanation is possible."

Thomas Aquinas –

Faith is not an Option!

The **Second Pillar** of a Rich man in Training is **Faith**. No matter what religion you practice, philosophy you follow, or belief system you may have, faith is at the root of it all. **Faith is not an Option**. It is a prerequisite that is required to develop the conditions, which attracts the very elements that generate riches in all areas of your life.

But what is faith? We commonly see faith tied directly to religion or a theistic tradition. However, faith is not the result of religion; religion is the result of faith. It's an interpretation of reality. It's a conviction of truth. Notice, I say it's a conviction. When someone is convicted, it has already happened. If your faith has the conviction of truth, in your mind, it has already happened, and you harbor no doubts. With this level of faith, you can change any condition, alter any reality, and develop the conditions necessary for riches to come into your life. As the great Martin Luther King, Jr. said, "Faith is taking the first step, even when you don't see the whole staircase."

"Faith is to believe what you do not see; the reward of this Faith is to see what you believe."

Saint Augustine–

Reward of Faith

In 2008, I met one of wealthiest men I personally know. It's safe to say, his net worth is well over half a billion US dollars; more importantly, he has built a legacy greater than his fortune. From what I gathered he's not particularly a religious man, but he's deeply spiritual. The level of faith he holds is without doubt, one of the greatest I've witnessed. Whenever he spoke to me about his vision and goals, he always spoke as if it had already happened. He left no doubt in my mind, that what he said would come to pass, even if it were something he planned years down the road. The conviction he held in his every word left no doubt to those he spoke to.

One day while I was sitting in his home office, overlooking the manicured lawns and lavish gardens, through window panes that encased his entire home office, I gathered the nerve to ask him, "How did he become so financially successful?" I remember how nervous I felt when I asked him this question. I heard he was a very private man and extremely protective of his privacy – however, I had to know. I had to know how he became so financially successful?

After I asked him the question, he cracked a pleasant smile and said, "You must have enough faith to believe you'll get what you want."

So, I asked him how so? He went on and told me in the 1970's, he had a vision that the land in Northwest Riverside

Faith is not an Option!

County, California, was going to become very valuable one day, because the neighboring County of Orange, was quickly running out of land to build new homes and communities. He believed that the next, logical area for the home builders to build, would be on this land. There was one major problem with the land at the time. It was zoned for agricultural use only, which meant the land could not be used to build homes. It could only be used for farming. This made the land useless in the minds of land developers and home builders, because the chances of the government re-zoning the land to build new homes on was very unlikely. With all the facts, he had faith that one day the laws would change and the land would be re-zoned for residential and commercial use, which would make the land extremely valuable when it did change. He continued to put together the finances he needed to purchase a great portion of this land, putting himself and his family at a huge financial risk. If this land did not get re-zoned, he stood to lose everything he had worked for.

Over the course of the next years, he maintained the land by farming it and selling the fruit he grew. The money he made from the sales of the fruit was just enough to pay the expenses, taxes, and the financing he used to purchase the land, which kept his investment safe. Over the years, he patiently waited for the land to be re-zoned for residential use. Year after year, all requests and petitions to re-zone the land failed – it was not looking good.

Rich Man in Training

Many years passed and his financial situation became unstable, as the taxes on the land raised and the income from his farms slowed down. The circumstances forced him to use his personal finances to continue paying for the expenses, taxes, and financing of the land. This situation rapidly worsened as his personal finances dwindled away and he was on the brink of bankruptcy.

At this point, he had to make a serious decision to sell the land, or stand by his faith – knowing the land will be re-zoned. His family begged him to sale the land as the threat to lose everything become greater with every passing day, but he maintained his faith. He knew without a doubt that this land would be re-zoned for residential property and he would make him a wealthy man.

His family literally thought he lost his mind, as they watched him edge closer to bankruptcy. Everyone around him thought he was being reckless with his decision to hold fast to his faith, and hold on to the land. Everything naturally pointed to him losing it all, but his Faith told him otherwise, so he firmly held on.

When he was nearly flat broke, and looking at a definite bankruptcy, the land was inexplicably re-zoned for residential use after dozens of failed attempts. As soon as the land was re-zoned, it did exactly as he expected. The value of the land sky rocketed. With the re-evaluation of the land, he could secure the funding he needed to develop it for homebuilders, increasing its value even more.

Faith is not an Option!

Once the land was developed he sold it and collected a fortune. This fortune provided the finances he needed to make other investments, which has built him a wildly successful portfolio of businesses, properties, and investments, which have cumulated a significant fortune over the years. Needleless to say, this fortune will support generations of his family to come, because he was rewarded for his faith.

Conviction in Faith

When you hold conviction in your faith, you are already saying it is done. Faith is the root that grows riches in all areas of life. It's your conviction. If you already except your riches as your truth, not a want, wish, or hope, it will become your reality.

Case example, when you mail a letter, you have undoubtable faith the letter will get to its destination. You won't give it a second thought, because you dropped the letter in the mail box. Correct?

Let's think about this. You drop a piece of mail in a blue box outside of your local Post Office. Then a postal worker gathers all the mail, and dumps it into a sorting bin, where it will get sorted by the zip code of the address it's going to, with thousands of others pieces of mail. Once it's sorted, it's bagged and transported to a processing center. After it is processed, it's delivered to the Post Office that will deliver the piece of mail to its destination.

During this whole process, there are so many possibilities that would prevent your letter from getting to its destination; It could get routed to the wrong Post Office; It could get lost at the process center; It could get eating up by the sorting machine; nevertheless, we have complete faith that none of these possibilities will prevent your letter from getting to its destination. In cases where we have a slight doubt, we pay a little bit of money to get the letter certified so it can be tracked. Although you have paid a higher price for assurance, the piece of mail will go through the same process to get delivered as the regular stamped mail, but again, we have complete faith with conviction that the letter will get to its destination. Do you see where this is going?

Most people have more faith in a cast of postal workers delivering their piece of mail, than they do in their own ability to obtain riches. It sounds silly, but it's the truth. We have more faith in strangers, than we do in defining our truth and claiming what is naturally ours, in riches. This lack of faith is the root to why so many of us remain broke in relationships, finances, career, health, spirit, mind, and ultimately life – the lack faith – the lack conviction.

Every rich man and women I've had the pleasure of meeting, all practice the conviction of faith. They all have infinite faith no matter their religion, background, nationality, or gender. They all have infinite faith. They believe without a doubt, and full conviction, they can have whatever they want. Some call this evidence a miracle; Some call it divine intervention; Some refer to it as the law of attraction. Whatever the case may be, faith is the root to all riches and there is no substitute – it is a requirement. I've been standing on faith for some time now, and it's taken me from a broken man's prison cell to enjoying my personal riches.

"Believe in yourself! Have Faith in your abilities! Without a humble but reasonable confidence in your own powers you cannot be successful or happy."

Norman Vincent Peale–

How do you hold conviction in Faith?

The question is, "How do you hold conviction in your faith?" The truth is we are born with it. If you watch a child, you'll see they have faith in all things. There is no doubt in the eyes of a child. They can day dream and live within that dream for hours. As we become an adult, the years of disappointments and challenges hinder our ability to have uninfluenced faith. We place limitations on ourselves. We stop believing in the unseen. We take everything with a grain of salt. We simply lose conviction and our faith along with it. We claim to have faith, but we are not willing to step out on it, let alone believe in it.

Rich men and women mastered the belief in their faith, holding it in absolute conviction, and channeling it into absolute truth. In their mind, their idea has already happened.

When my wife was in the early stages of her pregnancy, I declared with conviction, in my faith, our child was going to be a boy. Whenever I referenced our unborn child, I would lead with "he or his" before every sentence. I would start my dialogue off by saying, "His room…" or "He will…." My faith was so powerful, the conviction in my voice led my wife, daughter, in-laws, and parents to all reference our unborn child as "He". So, when my wife text me a photo of the ultrasound, I did not have to look at it. I already knew it was boy. I responded back to her text typing, "I told you it was a boy." There was never a doubt in my heart. I did not need an ultrasound to tell me what I already knew. My faith made it so.

It's so easy for us to have more faith in our limitations than in our abilities. Funny thing is that you can't see either. Your limitations are your reality, because you have more faith in the *limitations*, than your *ability* to obtain your riches. So, you'll continue to bring those conditions on yourself.

Learn to speak your desires into existence, through your faith. It's not just enough to speak it, you must believe it with absolute conviction. Speak of what things ought to be and not what they should not be. Everyday make it a habit to speak of things as if they have already happened. Not as if you are waiting on something to happen. If you speak on desires as a wish or a hope, it shows a clear lack of faith and conviction.

When I was in prison, I spoke of everything as if it had happened already. Knowing that one of my goals was to graduate college, these were the types of statements I would make.

After I graduate from college …

It was never

If I graduate college…

As an exercise, I want you to write 10 things that you wish to accomplish on your road to *Riches*. But I want you to write them as past tense. Meaning you have already accomplished it or it already has happened.

For example:
1. That's the sofa I will put in the living room, after I buy my house in June.

2. I plan on training for the marathon after I heal up from my surgery next week.

3. After we're married this summer, we're scheduled to visit Haiti for a mission trip.

4. After I'm the Vice President of the company, I'm going to change how the department is ran.

5. Next year, after we when the championship, we are going to the Bahamas.

After you write your 10 items. I want you to read them out loud daily and get used to hearing yourself say it. I want you to say it until you believe it, without a reasonable doubt. This is conviction and faith. It's a very powerful thing and will lead to you to your *True Riches*.

Faith is not an Option!

Keystones of the Pillar

1. Faith is a prerequisite to obtain your riches.

2. You must have conviction in your faith.

3. Speak of what things ought to be and not what they should not be.

4. You can have faith in your limitations or your abilities – not both.

Pillar III – What's Your Time Worth?

"Lost wealth may be replaced by industry, lost knowledge by study, lost health by temperance or medicine, but lost time is gone forever."

Samuel Smiles –

What's your time worth?

The **Third Pillar** of a Rich Man in Training is **Time Value**, or better put **What's your Time Worth?**

Rich men and women do not start their day with trivial tasks. They start following a precise schedule that protects their time. They know what their time is worth, and see it as an asset, like money to investments. Rich men and women avoid unproductive demands on their time, staying clear of time wasters. Each activity chosen, minute by minute, contributes to their goals and their riches.

Do you know *What your Time is Worth*? Is it $50 an hour? Is it $500 an hour? How much of your time are you spending on demands that have nothing to do with obtaining your *True Riches*? Do you know what those demands are costing you today? If you don't, you are doing yourself an injustice.

Imagine you spent the last 30 years preparing for your retirement, by investing your hard earn dollars into your company's 401K retirement plan. Every three months you receive a statement from the managing company of your 401K, explaining how well your investments are doing, and how much money you are accumulating for retirement.

Over the last 30 years, things have gone well with your 401K, and you've built it up to $976,000. You're happy with the idea you'll have a good amount of money invested to retire. One night while driving home from work, you hear a breaking news report that the CEO of the investment company managing your retirement fund, was just arrested for fraud and embezzlement. He has been stealing his clients' money for years in a large Ponzi Scheme. So, the next morning you rush and make some phone calls to check on your 401K, and you learn your $976,000 has been stolen. For the last 30 years, you've invested your money into a scheme. Of course, you can try to get the money back through legal channels, but for now your $976,000 is gone. It was all a fraud.

Think for a minute how devastated you would be, realizing you just lost $976,000. Think of how angry you would feel, knowing you've been swindled for the past 30 years. In essence, this is what you're doing to yourself when you don't know what your time is worth; when you are not investing your time to obtain your *True Riches*, you are swindling yourself. It's worst in your case, because you know you are not investing your time in what matters. You're not accounting for what your time is worth. If it was a crime to waste our time, how many of us would be in jail today? While we may not go to a physical prison, the quality of our lives becomes our prison; wishing for our *True Riches*, but never getting them.

So, I'll pose the question again, "What is your time worth? Is it $50 an hour? Is it $500 and hour? Are you investing your time to obtain your *True Riches*?" If not, don't fret. By the end of this chapter, you should know what your time is worth, and value every minute as an investment toward obtaining your *True Riches*.

What's your time worth?

Time Value

I've read numerous books on time management. These books focus on how to manage your time, how to become more efficient with your time, and the best books teach you how to avoid time wasters. These concepts are very important and will help you obtain your riches. Incidentally, there seems to be missing factor. Why do prestigious organizations like Harvard Business School take the time to publish books on time management? Why do CEOs, Entertainers, and Leaders pay professionals to help them manage their time and schedules? What is the priceless secret, not being told in these books?

Time is the most precious asset we have as human beings. We can't buy time back. We can't purchase more of it. We can't get a loan on it. Once time is spent, it's gone. No Exchange; No Refund; All Sales are Final.

In the banking and finance industries, they know the value of time. The most important concept in finance is the *Time Value of Money*, which is based on time. Hence the word "time" in *Time Value of Money*. The industry uses standard calculations to determine what the value of money is today, and what it would be worth 10 years from now, if they were to loan it out at X percent of interest. This calculation is heavily used to determine what types of investments the banks will make and how much money they will invest.

As an example, when we buy a car, most of us go to the dealership and find a car we like. Once we find the car we like, the dealership connects us with a bank to secure a loan for the purchase. From the banks perspective, they see the loan as an investment, and want to know what their return on their investment will be (how much they would make by loaning you the money) before they give you the loan. Two key factors they look at, outside of your credit and how much you can put down, is the term of the loan (how long the loan is for) and the interest rate of the loan (how much the bank is going to charge you to borrow the money). However, the true money maker for the bank is the term of the loan (how long is the loan for) – *Time Value of Money*. I will show you how this works.

Suppose a bank loans you $28,750, at 6% interest rate, to buy the car. You must determine if you want a 72-month loan or a 36-month loan (the time of the loan). After you calculate how much you'll pay for each loan, you realize that you would pay $2,722 more for the 72-month loan. Why is this? Everything is the same with the loan as far as we can tell. The interest rate of the loan is 6%. The amount of the loan is $28,750. The only difference is the term (time of the loan).

Term / Time	APR	Loan Amount	How much you'll pay
72 - Months	6%	$ 28,750	$ 34,272
36 - Months	6%	$ 28,750	$ 31,500
Difference			$ 2,772

What's your time worth?

The bank charges for every day you borrow their money; you are paying them for the borrowing time. The more time it takes you to pay them back, the more you must pay them for the loan. Therefore, you would pay them $34,272 for the 72-month loan, and $31,500 for the 36-month loan. You are paying them for *Time*.

When I learned this concept, I realized the *True Value* is not in money, it's in *Time*. If I were to take out a loan today and pay it back tomorrow, the loan would essentially cost me nothing; there would not be enough time for the interest to build up. Time determines everything. If we all could live forever, we all would eventually become multi-millionaires; unfortunately, we all have an expiration date; meaning, we are running out of time with every breath we take. Typing this sentence cost me five seconds; however, it's ok, because I'm investing it into one of my *True Riches* – Time well spent.

Statistics shows we live between 64 and 80 years on average, depending on gender, race, socioeconomic status, etc. On average, we live between 23,376 and 29,220 days. If you are middle age, you can cut this in half. You have between 11,688 to 14,610 left of your life to live. How will you spend your most precious asset? Do you even know what your most precious asset cost? I'm sure the bank would know, if they were in the business of selling time. On second thought, they do, with the *Time Value of Money* concept. So, think of your time as the **Time Value of Life**.

> *"We need a sense of the value of time – that is, of the best way to divide one's time into one's various activities."*
>
> *Arnold Bennett –*

What's your time worth?

Now that you understand Time Value, ask yourself, "What is my time worth?" If you are unsure, this section will assist you with that determination. For those who are certain of their value, this section will confirm your investment. You must think of your time as an investment. When you know how much your time is worth, you will know how to best invest it.

The first step to determine the value of your time, is to think of how much money you wish to earn, rather than what you are currently earning. Envision yourself making this amount of money. Do not be shy. If it's $100,000 a year, then it's a $100,000 a year. If it's a $1,000,000 a year, then it's a $1,000,000 a year. Have conviction in the amount you have chosen. Remember, faith with conviction leads to truth. Do not make it a fantasy number, because it will not work. Your time must hold true value. To calculate this value, you must believe that the dollar amount is real.

So, let's say you have decided you see yourself making $1,000,000 a year – Perfect! – we have a number. Let's

What's your time worth?

divide the $1,000,000 by how many hours there are in a year. There are 8,766 hours in each year, unless it's a leap year.

$$\$1{,}000{,}000 / 8{,}766 = \$114.08$$

The value of your time will calculate to **$114.08** per hour. Now, let's multiply this **$114.08** by **1.25**. Why are we multiplying the **$114.08** by **1.25**? Remember, your time is an investment. For every hour you spend (use or lose), it will cost you **$114.08**; however, you should expect to get something in return for your time. It's the future value of your time.

So, let's calculate the future value of your time.

$$\$114.08 \times 1.25 = \$142.60$$

$142.60 is what your time is worth per hour, based on your commitment to make a $1,000,000 a year.

To calculate the value of your time, you can download the "***Rich Man in Training – What's Your Time Worth Calculator***" from **richmanintraining.com** resources page.

RICH MAN
IN TRAINING
WHAT'S YOUR TIME WORTH CALCULATOR

How Much Do You want to Make a Year?

| Type in How Much You Want to Make a Year Here: | $ | 10,000,000.00 |
| This How Much Your Time is Worth Per Hour: | $ | 1,425.96 |

Time Study

As I explained earlier in this chapter, you can't buy additional time. Once you determine the value of your time, you will want to invest it wisely, reaping the best return. This is a concept that all rich men and women have mastered.

The first step in determining how to invest your time is through a time study. Time study is a record, recording where you spent your time. It's your personal report card that shows how well you've invested your most precious asset.

When I completed my first-time study in December 2011, I was stunned at how much of my time was being wasted on tasks and activities, which had nothing to do with helping me obtain my *True Riches*. Prior to me completing my time study, I thought I did a great job investing my time into activities geared to reaching my goals. From the point of being released from prison, to this moment in time, I made a lot of accomplishments. Although, when I reviewed my time study, I noticed I was not investing enough time in obtaining my *True Riches*. Nearly every waken moment was invested into my career. This was apparent as my career excelled and my income vastly increased; however, my career was not my *True Riches*. I considered my *True Riches* to be my marriage, children, family, health, spirituality, and meaningful relationships.

Completing my time study allowed me to take inventory of my life. It was clear as to why I was having trouble with my marriage and feeling a sense of disconnect with my family; my moral compass was broken and I began to feel like that broken man again. Because all my time was spent on my career, I didn't have much of it left to spend with my wife and daughter; days would pass with only a few "Good Mornings" being spoken, and I had not seen my parents in weeks. I spent a lot of time with my associates doing what they wanted to do, in efforts to become part of the upper echelon.

As a result of my time study, I was able to see how poorly I invested my time. I gave myself a "D-" on my report card. I realized I was investing most of my time in activities that had nothing to do with me obtaining my *True Riches*. I was building a career that could have ended at any moment. I was investing my time with people that did not have my best interest at heart. If I kept on the same road, I was going to end up investing 30 years of my time into a Ponzi Scheme. I was robbing myself.

Doing your Time Study

To begin your time study, you will want to record your time by documenting your activities in ten-minute increments. Start recording your activities from the moment you wake up, and ending the second you prepare to go to sleep. Ideally you should do the time study from two to four weeks. This will provide enough information to study how you are investing your time. The longer you do the study, the better reporting you'll get. Below is a sample of one of my time study.

You can download the *"Rich Man in Training – Time Study Worksheet"* from **richmanintraining.com** resources page.

Time	Sun	Mon	Tue
5:00 PM	Bio break	checked phone messages	Dinner
5:10 PM	Took call from book editor	Called back editor	Dinner
5:20 PM	Got tea	Called back TRU Statement Inc. VP	Checked Emails
5:30 PM	Read manuscript	Called back mom	Responded to emails
5:40 PM	Read manuscript	Drive home	Responded to emails
5:50 PM	Read manuscript	Drive home	Responded to emails

What's your time worth?

After your time study is complete, look at each time entry and ask yourself, "What did this task contribute to my goals?" Be open and honest with yourself. This is the only way you will be able to determine if you are getting the best return on your investment of time. It's your report card.

Once you determine if your activities bring you closer to your riches, ask yourself if you could have done more with your time to get even closer to your Riches. If you see something in the time study that appeared to be a time waster, ask yourself the question, "What could I have done differently, to avoid this time waster?"

For example, a friend calls you to ask a valid question. Then the conversation moves on from the question to a conversation about the controversial views on the Presidential Election. This conversation goes on for another 15 minutes, with your friend expressing their political views.

This conversation is what I would consider a time waster. You just invested 15 minutes in a conversation that had nothing to do with you obtaining your *True Riches*. There is nothing you could do to change the election. At this point, you are two-people gossiping.

Think about all the other things you could have accomplished with that 15 minutes you can't get back. You could have been, reading or listening to a book, working on a business plan, writing your book, or talking to your spouse about ideas and the future you want. You simply could have been using that time to obtain your *True Riches*.

Keeping a Schedule

Now that you know the value of time and what your time is worth, you must ask yourself, "How do I effectively manage it?"

Scheduling! Scheduling! Scheduling!

As odd as it may seem, I discovered the importance of scheduling while I was in prison. Every moment of my day was set on a schedule; the time I could take a shower, go to chow, call my family, get a haircut, work out, etc..... If you missed the scheduled time to do any of these things, you simply didn't do them. There was no, "I'm sorry for being late."

In prison, the most important thing scheduled, outside of your release date, is when you can go to the canteen (store) to purchase goods. Every month there is a draw that schedules each inmates date and time, as to when they can go to the store to purchase food, bathing soap, cigarettes, toothpaste, and other goods. If you miss your draw, you would have to go without goods for another month. This resulted in bartering for the items you need or borrowing items from another inmate at an extremely high interest rate.

Every month I would see dozens of inmates miss their draw, for whatever reason. This was evident, because every day I would see an inmate pleading his case to the officer in

What's your time worth?

charge of the canteen, as to why he missed his scheduled appointment to purchase his goods. He would stand their begging the officer to give him another opportunity to go to the store. It was a bit embarrassing to see a grown man begging another person to let him buy a stick of deodorant.

When I saw this, I decided to open my own store. During my scheduled draw, I purchased several extra items to loan other inmates at the going prison rate, which was at 100% interest. This meant, they would have to give you back two items for every one item they borrowed.

I was beside myself, by the fact that I could count on the same inmates to miss their draw month after month, and turn around to pay me double for what they could have bought at the canteen just as I did. All they had to do was show up to the canteen at their scheduled time to purchase their goods. However, they could not keep a schedule and always ended up paying double for what they wanted or needed. It was rib-tickling every time I thought about this. They had nothing better to do but to keep their schedule, but since they could not, they paid the penalty.

Sadly, this is exactly what happens every day to those who do not keep a schedule. They are penalized, but far worst then having to pay double for a toiletry item. They are penalized with a mediocre life. They are unable to maintain employment, they lack meaningful relationships, they have poor health, their spiritualty is constantly challenged, they lack faith, they lack confidence, their life stays in constant turmoil.

I have found the most successful people in the world operate off a set schedule. Every portion of their day is scheduled on their calendar. Phone calls, meetings, drive time, family time, gym time, all times. If it's not on their schedule, it does not exist. This is how your Beyoncés, Bill Gates, Tony Robbins, Stephen Currys of the world live their lives. Many of these well-known figures higher assistances, whose sole job is to manage their schedule and keep them on task. Rich Men and Women of the world understand this and maintain a consistent practice on keeping a schedule.

Effective Scheduling

Over the course of the past decade, I've worked diligently at improving how I managed my day through effective scheduling, which helped me get the most out of my time. I've used various methods that I learned from Harvard Business School, Peter Drucker, Kevin Kruse, and Stephen Convey. I tested each method through trial and error until I fined tuned a method that works well for me.

The system I developed helped me graduate from college with honors, spend time with my children, enjoy my marriage, effectively build a career, sit on the board of non-profit organizations, mentor at-risk teens, counsel young married couples, host workshops at the local university, build new positive relationships, write this book, and continue my

What's your time worth?

education. Not too bad for a high school drop out that spent his late teens and first half of his twenties incarcerated.

To maintain an effective schedule that will help you obtain your Riches, you must schedule the most important tasks in your life first, before scheduling anything else. It makes no point in scheduling things that does not contribute to your road to Riches first.

To do this, you must determine what you want to accomplish each day, week, month, quarter, and year based on the Riches you seek.

In chapter one, we went through the exercise of creating your list of *True Riches*, goals, and tasks. We'll now take this list of tasks and schedule them on a calendar.

On the following pages, I have given you an example of a few of my task list and a calendar showing how each item is scheduled.

Riches in Marriage:
Goal: Provide my wife love and encouragement. Bring us closer to one another.

    A. **Daily Task:** Spend time listening to my wife's thoughts
    B. **Daily Task:** Give my wife daily words of affirmation.
    C. **Weekly Task:** Write my wife a love letter
    D. **Month:** Take my wife on a dinner date

Riches in my Children:
Goal: Develop my son and daughter into thought leaders and contributors to society.

    A. **Daily Task:** Talk to my teenage daughter for 30 minutes, to discuss what's going on in her life and transfer my knowledge to her.
    B. **Weekly Task:** Spend at least 4 hours per week with my toddler son teaching him his abc's, numbers, and words.
    C. **Month:** Teach my daughter how to drive on the freeway.

What's your time worth?

Riches in Health:
Goal: Maintain good physical and mental health
- A. **Daily Task:** Take my vitamins
- B. **Daily Task:** Meditate for at least 10 minutes each morning
- C. **Daily Task:** Sleep at least 6 hours per day
- D. **Weekly Task:** Work out at least 4 hours per week
- E. **Month:** Go for a hike in Big Bear

Note: Each of your Riches should be broken out specifically in a form like you see above.

Now that you have your list of tasks ready to schedule, determine what type of calendar you wish to use. I personally use Microsoft Outlook as my calendar. However, there are several other types of electronic calendars that work well; and of course, the handy daily planner is a great option.

You can download the *"**Rich Man in Training – Daily Planner**"* from **richmanintraining.com** resources page, to help you with your scheduling.

Two things I suggest that your calendar or planner should have:

1. A section on the calendar that you can write in your task list. In my Outlook, it is at the bottom of my calendar.
2. A color code or each item on your schedule, to determine what each schedule item is contributing to on your road to Riches.

On the next page, I've provide a snapshot of my Calendar for the first week of December 2016.

What's your time worth?

◀ ▶ December 4 - 10, 2016   Los Angeles, California ▾

	SUNDAY 4	MONDAY 5	TUESDAY 6
12 AM			
1			
2			
3			
4			
5		Meditate	Meditate
6		Work out at GYM	Work out at GYM
7		Talk to Daughter, while	Talk to Daughter, while
8			
9		Meeting with Editor	
10	Brunch with Family		
11			
12 PM		Lunch	
1	Spend Time with Son	Meeting with TRU - CEO	
2			
3		Pick Daughter up from Scl	
4			
5			
6	Family Dinner		
7			
8	Write Article		
9	Chat with wife		
10	Review my schedule for th		
11			

Show tasks on: Due Date

Tasks:
- Speak to daughter
- Spend time speakin...
- Give wife daily word...
- Take vitamins
- Meditate for 10 min...

Keystones of the Pillar

1. Time is your most precious asset. You must learn to invest it, in what matters.

2. Maintain a set schedule by scheduling everything in your life. This will help you avoid time wasters and prune unproductive activities.

3. Complete a time study at least once a quarter. It's your report card on how well you are investing your time.

4. Review your schedule daily and confirm that you stayed on tasks.

Pillar IV – Live Intentional

"I want to be intentional about my freedom – in choosing it, honoring it, and protecting it. One of the best feelings I know is feeling truly free."

Kristin Armstrong –

Live Intentional

The **Fourth Pillar** of a Rich Man in Training is **Live Intentional.** This means to be committed at all that you do. Set the expectation. You can't tolerate sitting on the fence or guessing your way through life. You must be calculated, conscious, planned, and purposeful. Always know what you want and commit to it. Live with Intent.

This world has approximately 4 billion people in it. Most of the 4 billion are not living a life full of *Riches* and enrichment. They are living a life that is managed, dictated, or controlled by someone else. Their life is controlled by another person's agenda or intentions. It's the old saying, if you don't choose, someone else will choose for you. Sadly, a large amount of us allow someone else to choose for us.

Ask yourself honest questions. Why have you chosen to do what you are doing today? Why are you working the job you are working? Why do you live where you live? Why do you have the education you have? Why is your child going to the school he/she is going to? Were any of your choices *Intentional*? Was it your plan, or are you a part of someone else's plan? Take a few minutes and think about it.

"Your time is limited, so don't waste it living someone else's life. Don't be trapped by dogma – which is living with the results of other people's thinking. Don't let the noise of others' opinions drown out you own inner voice. And most important, have the courage to follow your heart and intuition."

Steve Jobs -

Rich Men and Women are always *Intentional*. They do not ask for permission to obtain their *Riches*. They are not waiting for some life circumstance to give them purpose. They are not living someone else's life. They live in conviction. All of which they do is calculated and intended. They create their own circumstances. They create the conditions to bring them *Riches*. They are the winning lottery ticket.

The Entrepreneur

One afternoon I had lunch with a successful entrepreneur to discuss a project. During our lunch, we began discussing our children and our intentions to help them succeed at life, by giving them all the advantages possible. During our conversation, he brought up what schools he wanted his one-year old daughter to attend for elementary, middle, and high school.

Live Intentional

He told me about a private elementary school that he went to in an upper middle-class city outside of Los Angeles. He attributed his success to the quality of the education he received at this school, and wanted the same level of education for his daughter. He explained how the school set grand expectations on all their students with an advance curriculum, which set the foundation for him to become the accomplished man he was today.

Based on his intentions to have his daughter go to this school, he laid out his plan to sale his home and build a new home near the school he wanted his daughter to attend. Then he went on to discuss his plan for the next five years, regarding everything from his business interests to his family. Every aspect of his life was planned with intention. He was very calculated and you knew he was *Intentional* in all that he did. He created circumstances and was not controlled by them. I could tell he would not tolerate anything less.

What will you Tolerate?

For one to *Live Intentional*, you must have set expectations. Identify your set expectations as what you are willing to tolerate. What you expect and what you tolerate, are the two sides of the same coin. What do I mean by this?

Let's say, every two weeks you receive the same paycheck of $800 dollars. This income is not enough for you and your family to live on; however, you continue to work this job year in and year out, tolerating these conditions. Your spouse knows this is your income. There is no expectation for you to bring home any more money, neither are you. It's what you've accepted by tolerating the conditions of a $800 paycheck. It's your unspoken expectations.

This would hold true if you were a professional athlete, lawyer, doctor, or a convenience store worker. The conditions they tolerate becomes their unspoken expectation. For an athlete or a lawyer, they do not tolerate losing. Their expectation is to win. The day they start to tolerate losing, is the day they need to consider another profession. For a doctor, they do not tolerate an unnecessary loss of life. Their expectation is to help heal people through their knowledge of medicine. If they lose this expectation, I pray they quit right away!

Let's pause here for a quick exercise. I would like you to write down 7 current things or areas in your life that you are tolerating. Be open and honest. Is it your salary? Is it your child's bad grades? Is it your level of education? Is it the neighborhood you live in? Is it your health? Is it an addiction of some sort?

After you write out your list on what you are tolerating, I want you to write new expectations are for each of the items. See the example on the next page.

Tolerate	Expectation
I tolerate making $2,700 every two weeks	I expect to make $4,000 every two weeks
I tolerate my son getting "Cs" in school	I expect my son to get "Bs" or better in school
I tolerate my car not starting in the morning	I expect my car to start in the morning
I tolerate being an employee	I expect to own my own business
I tolerate my high cholesterol	I expect to be healthy
I tolerate living in a high crime neighborhood	I expect to live in a safe and peaceful neighborhood
I tolerate drinking every night	I expect to wake up focused and fresh and not feeling sluggish in the morning

After writing down your expectations, take a few minutes and look over the list. See if your expectations match what you are tolerating. If what you are tolerating is less than what you expect, then there is some work to do to meet those expectations. Otherwise, you've accepted your conditions for what they are, and what you are tolerating is truly your unspoken expectations. You are not *Living Intentional*. You have allowed circumstances to dictate how you live your life.

So, you have a choice here. You can either close this book and continue to tolerate your circumstances, or you can put an action plan together to meet your expectations.

The Action Plan

The first three Pillars of a Rich Man in Training are Know thy Riches, Faith is not an Option, and What's your Time Worth. These areas are a prerequisite to helping you develop an action plan to *Live Intentional*. It is your compass – sort to speak. At this point you know what you want. There is no debating that. You've identified your *True Riches*. You understand that you must have conviction through Faith, and you know what you time is worth. You must now act on it.

For each expectation, you've set for yourself, you must claim your intention to meet that expectation. Next to each listed expectation, I want you to write down what you intend to do to meet that expectation. I've provided an example below.

Expectation	Intentions
I expect to make $4,000 every two weeks	I will increase my income to $4,000 every two weeks
I expect my son to get "Bs" or Better in school	I will help my son improve his grades to a "B" or higher
I expect my car to start in the morning	I will purchase a new car July of next year
I expect to own my own business	I will start my own business in 2 years
I expect to be healthy	I will lose 20 pounds in 12 months
I expect to live in a nice neighborhood	I will buy a house in a better neighborhood in two years
I expect to wake up focused and fresh and not feeling sluggish in the morning	Today I will stop drinking nightly

Now that you've made you've stated your intentions. Now What? It's time to commit!

> *"Unless commitment is made, there are only promises and hopes…. but no plans"*
>
> *Perter Drucker -*

What's Intentions without Commitment?

In the quote by Peter Drucker, he explains that unless you commit there is only hope and no plans. Think of your Expectations as the Hope and your Intentions as the Promise. Understanding, however, they both mean nothing without commitment. You must commit!

When you commit to something, you're making a promise to meet expectations. You are being *Intentional*. You are not asking for permission. You are setting the condition to obtain your *Riches*. You are placing yourself into a binding contract. In business, if one fails to keep their commitment it may end up in court. In marriage, if you fail to keep your commitments it may end up in divorce. If one fails to keep a commitment to a moral standard, who knows where they may end up – jail, destitute, or death? For you, failing to keep your commitments does not result in just failing yourself, it results in you failing everyone who depends on you. Your stock goes down each time you fail to commit and it goes down even more when you do not come through on your commitments. You can have all the intentions in the world, but it means nothing without your commitment to them.

Live Intentional

Have you ever trusted someone to do something for you and they failed to keep their commitment? What were your honest thoughts about that person? Exactly! It would come to the point that the only thing you trust about that person, is that they do not keep their commitments.

Take a closer look at yourself, how often have you failed to keep your commitments? Think about how you would see yourself, if you were the person not keeping the commitment to yourself. You would see yourself as you would see the person who failed to keep their commitments.

A great way to keep your commitments is with an accountability partner. So, what's an accountability partner? An accountability partner, is the person(s) that you can trust to help you stay committed to your intentions and focused on your *Riches*. This person or persons, knows what your *True Riches* are. They know what your goals are. They know what your commitments are. For me, it's my wife. I've given her the permission to hold me accountable, always. I expect her to hold me accountable. If she sees me watching TV, when I should be preparing for a workshop, she calls me out on it. When she notices that I'm not keeping my calendar, she calls me out on it. Even if it's a very small item, she reminds me what may seem small to me, may be all the difference between me obtaining my *Riches* or not.

As a task, I want you to find yourself an accountability partner. Someone close enough to you, that you can freely share the *Riches* you intend to obtain. I want you to write a letter to this person, describing your *True Riches*, goals, and intentions. This letter will stand as your personal contract with them. In this letter ask them to hold you accountable. Give them permission to keep you honest and on your road to *Riches*. Think of them as your personal manager. After you write the letter, go over it with them and ask if they would be willing to help you. If they agree, you both should sign the letter as a binding contract. If you need help with writing your accountability letter you can download the **"Rich Man in Training – Accountability Pledge Letter - Template"** from **richmanintraining.com** resources page as a guide.

Once your accountability letter is signed, immediately schedule a weekly call or meeting with your accountability partner(s), to discuss your progress with them. You must be open and honest in these conversations. It is important to understand, if you are not open and honest, you are not deceiving them, you are deceiving yourself. The point of this exercise is to ensure that you keep your commitments and that you are living an Intentional life.

Live Intentional

Keystones of the Pillar

1. Live an Intentional life. You must be calculated, conscious, planned, and purposeful.

2. You don't have to ask for permission to obtain your *Riches*. You don't have to wait for circumstance to occur to obtain your *Riches*. You create the circumstances.

3. What you chose to tolerate are your true expectations.

4. Unless you commit to your intentions, they remain as promises and not material reality.

Pillar V - Working Knowledge

"When a man's knowledge is not in order, the more of it he has the greater will be his confusion."

Herbert Spencer –

Working Knowledge

The **Fifth Pillar** of a Rich Man in Training is effectively using knowledge to obtain your *True Riches*. This knowledge is called **Working Knowledge.** The reason I say *Working Knowledge*, is because it's not enough to just have the knowledge to obtain your *True Riches*. You must use the knowledge you have to obtain your *True Riches*. It's putting your knowledge to work or *Working Knowledge.*

How many times have we heard the story about a college graduate working at McDonald's? Then turn around and hear a story about a high school dropout who became a multimillionaire? What was so special about the high school dropout? He was no more gifted than the college graduate? In fact, he may have been at a disadvantaged in terms of education; however, he took the knowledge he had and put it to work. I've seen this first hand on many occasions. An example comes to mind of two different men I had the pleasure of meeting.

The first was a young man who grew up very poor. When he was 12 years old, he and his younger brother would sell fruit on the side of the road, hoping to earn money to help their parents pay the bills. By the time he was a teenager, his friends were all associated with the local gangs, and he was stuck in the middle of the madness. Fortunately, he escaped the madness long enough to be introduced to a man, who shared with him the knowledge of how to start his own financial services business.

At first, the young man balked at the idea, of starting his own financial services business. He believed someone from his background couldn't do such a thing. He had no college degree. He had no background in finances. He barely graduated high school. How could he become capable of helping families build financial plans, when he, himself, had no money?

However, the 19-year-old was introduced to a very successful broker in the business, and learned that this broker came from a similar poverty-stricken background. Amazed at the possibilities, he asked the broker to teach him how to build his own business.

The broker advised him to clean himself up by dressing business appropriate, and do all that he asked of him to do, and he would help him. The young man agreed to the terms and got started immediately.

Over the course of the next couple years, he did exactly as the broker taught him, and put his new knowledge to work as fast as he received it. By the time he was in his mid-twenties, he had established one of the fastest growing financial services businesses in his area, generating a personal income of over quarter million dollars a year. When he turned 29, his personal income was over a million dollars a year.

What I learned about this young man, was that he became a master at working his knowledge. Whatever he learned, he immediately put it to work. He didn't wait or guess. He quickly started working his knowledge. He became so skilled at doing this, he could digest a great amount of information and quickly use it as his *working knowledge.*

Outside of the financial rewards earned from working his knowledge, he brought his family out of their financial hardships and has built a secure foundation for them all.

From what I know of this young man, he has become a beacon of hope for all those around him and enriches the lives of every individual he encounters. When I met him, you would have thought he was a Financial Engineer, because of how well he articulated himself and understood the financial services business. He simply put his knowledge to work!

On the other hand, the second young man was a well-educated person that was stuck in a rut. He had every advantage over the first young man, but failed to put his knowledge to work.

While the first young man was hustling fruit bags on the side of roads, the 2nd young man was attending a prestigious boarding school, getting a top-level education. After graduating from the boarding school, he went on to a prestigious college and graduated with a Bachelor's degree in business. After obtaining his Bachelor's degree, he went on to management school and received his Master in Business Administration (MBA). You could say that he received the best education money could buy.

All though he had all this education, he did not put his knowledge to work. When I met him, it was right after he graduated with his MBA. At that time, he was working an entry level accounting clerk job. The position was meant for an intern or data entry person. The position was not meant for a someone educated with an MBA in business. It was apparent he knew this, because he would always express his dissatisfaction of not being able to use his knowledge. When I asked him what he desired most, he told me he wanted to open his own marketing company. I deeply believed he could have done so. When it came to marketing, he was one of the most gifted minds I had ever come across at that time. He was like a walking encyclopedia for the world of marketing. He could tell me just about anything on the subject; however, he was not working the knowledge. He was working a mindless job.

What I noticed about the 2nd young man, is that he had the tendency to over analyze everything. He had to validate everything by comparing it to the education he had. This did nothing more than confuse him. It was apparent that he had the intelligence and knowledge he needed, but lack the imagination in working with his knowledge. He would sit at his desk and poke at something for hours, to never act on it. It was like watching a cat play with a mouse until it died. Think of the mouse as the opportunity and he kept clawing at it until it was lifeless and died.

Working Knowledge

"The True sign of intelligence is not knowledge but imagination."

Albert Einstein –

Using Working Knowledge

Today it's commonly known that data is turned into information. Information informs us of something that we can use for our knowledge. We use our knowledge for common things, like taking an umbrella out when we know it's going to rain. This is what I refer to as general knowledge. It doesn't take much to use it, it's our second nature.

On the other hand, *Working Knowledge* exercises your intelligence. It takes imagination to use it. It's like building a puzzle. You can see the picture on the box, which gives you an idea of what the puzzle is going to look like when you are finished. It's now up to you to figure out how to build it.

You don't have to be formally educated to build the puzzle. This is where I hear so many people stop. They think you must have some special knowledge to move on. You just have to know how to use what resources you have available. In this case, it's the area you are going to use to build your puzzle (where are you are going to use your knowledge), the pieces of the puzzle (each piece represents a bit of your knowledge) and your imagination (how you are going to use your knowledge to build the puzzle).

When you begin to build your puzzle the first thing is use what you know. We know that all the pieces with one flat side, is commonly the edge of the puzzle. So, we group them all together and use them to build the puzzle's border.

The next thing we do is look for the pieces with similar colors and group them together. Once we group the pieces together, we then begin building the puzzle from the edges, by determining what pieces fit together. When you hit a road block, you then start to work on another area of the puzzle. Continuous progress is better than delayed perfection. You keep on moving forward until you complete the puzzle.

What you've done is what Rich Men and Women have been doing for years. They put their knowledge to work to complete life's puzzles. They don't set on their knowledge and wonder about it. They piece it together and complete the puzzle.

As an exercise, I would like you to buy a 500-piece puzzle and put it together. Personalize it. For example, purchase a puzzle with beautiful scenery where you may want to take a future dream vacation. As you strategize on how to best match the pieces, relate it to how you will work your knowledge to take this dream trip. Or take a photo of your love ones to a print shop, and have the photo made into a

Working Knowledge

puzzle. As you work your knowledge to fit the pieces together, it will be a reminder of what you are working towards. Your *True Riches*!

> *"Employ your time in improving yourself by other men's writings, so that you shall gain easily what others have labored hard for"*
>
> *Socrates–*

Sources of Knowledge

Knowledge comes to us in many different forms. Knowledge may be received from formal education (school), informal education (self-taught), mentoring, workshops, seminars, coaches, and life experiences. These sources of knowledge hold an infinite amount of value. The knowledge I obtained from a person with a life sentence in prison, was just as important as the knowledge I obtained from one of my college professors.

Never blindly disregard a source of knowledge, based on some preconceived notion that good knowledge comes from an expert, genius, or academia. Be open and willing to listen, to whomever is willing to share knowledge with you. You're never too smart to listen. As a naive young man, I made this mistake, more times than I could count. I can say this mistake cost me over a million dollars – I'll explain how.

In 1996, at the age of 15, I was selling drugs in the back alley of a liquor store. Every night, a customer, we'll call Dave, would buy $150 dollars' worth of crack cocaine from me. I would always wonder where he got his money from, because he was the poster child for a crackhead. Dave was a very thin middle age man, that smelled something terrible, and looked like he had been living on the streets for years. His eyes were always bugged out, clothes very dirty, and his lips was always dry and cracked.

Every evening, like clockwork, Dave would show up to purchase his fix for the night, and disappear behind an old abandoned factory. One night, around 2am, I decided to move my operation behind the old factory.

When I arrived behind the factory, I saw my customer Dave sitting on a stairway smoking the rock cocaine I sold him earlier that evening. After sitting there with him for 15 minutes, another customer located me and bought $40 dollars' worth of crack. Just before I could put the money in my pocket, Dave asked, "So, how much money do you make a night?"

Defensively I said, "None of your business!"

Dave continued with asking, "How would you like to become a millionaire?"

I laughed and quickly disregarded his statement, as an old junky just ranting on like all the others.

Over the next hour, he kept nudging me to listen to him. He told me that he was a banker and he could teach me how to make a million dollars. I thought to myself, the only thing he could show me was how to hit a crack pipe. However, he insisted that he wanted show me how I could make a million dollars. After a while, I gave in and decided to entertain him and listen to his million-dollar scheme.

Over the next 41 minutes, he explained some wild idea on how I could invest my money in a way that would become a million dollars by the time I was 50. I heckled him the entire time, which agitated him to the point he stopped to scold me by saying, "Look you fucking idiot, I made my first million before I was 30, and I became a multimillionaire before I was 40. Now, you can listen to me or end up shot dead out here like the rest of your homeboys!"

So, I silenced myself until he was done showing me how I could make a million dollars. Sure, I was hearing him, but not really listening. He might as well have been talking to a wall. I could not get past the fact he was a crackhead living on the streets. After our conversation, I didn't think much about what he said, and wrote off our conversation as another junky telling a good story.

Then in 2009, while sitting in my corporate finance class, at California State University, San Bernardino, the professor began the class by saying he was going to show us how we could all make a million dollars with the right low risk investments, based on the concept of compound interest. My ears perked up, because the statement had sounded so familiar.

Within the first 10 minutes of the lesson, my mouth dropped open in disbelief. The professor wrote out the same exact formula on the whiteboard, that Dave the crackhead scribbled on a rotten piece of cardboard, sitting under a flickering light, while crack smoke flowed from his mouth. I couldn't believe it! Dave really knew what he was talking about. The funny thing about it, he explained the concept better than the college professor. I sat for the rest of the class doing calculations on how much money I could have had, if I listened to Dave 13 years ago. That number came to a figure just north of a million dollars.

From that day forward, I no longer discount the knowledge that someone shares with me, because of the source. I don't care if the knowledge comes from a waiter at a restaurant or a vagrant who is asking me for change. If the information they provide me is pertinent and can add to my knowledge, I give it enough respect to investigate it and determine if it's worth considering further.

You'll be very surprised where your knowledge may come from. In most cases, the best knowledge you receive will come from the most unlikely places or from a most unexpected source. It's your responsibility to quickly determine its worth and put it to work – if you plan to be a Rich Man.

"As knowledge increases, wonder deepens"

Charles Morgan –

Knowledge is a Life Long Journey

Years ago, I was told knowledge is not a trip, it's a journey. When you stop obtaining knowledge your journey will end. I recognized the truth in this statement as I began to build my knowledge and put it to work. The more I succeeded in life, the more I wanted to know. The more I knew, the greater the possibilities to obtain my *True Riches*.

Knowledge does not stop at an experience or after you received a degree or certificate. This is where the journey begins.

Think about a young man, who one day wants to become a heart surgeon. He begins his life long journey in the knowledge of medicine as early as 16 years old. He begins his journey by working in a hospital and studying biology in high school. He moves on to college as a pre-med major. As a pre-med major, he invests four years at a University preparing for medical school, by volunteering at a hospital, doing pre-med course work, and obtaining clinical experience; all of which is adding to the knowledge he received in high school.

After he graduates from college, he takes the accumulation of his knowledge and prepares for the MCAT, an entrance exam for medical school. Once he passes the MCAT exam, he can now apply for medical school. Up to this point, all the knowledge obtained was just to apply for medical school. He now has four remaining years to build his knowledge to qualify for graduation, to become a medical doctor and begin his career.

    This young man has invested over 10 years of his life towards the journey of knowledge, with the intent to officially practice medicine.

    Once he graduates from medical school, he then must prepare to take the medical board exam that will grant him a license to practice medicine. After passing the board exam, he will be required to do a residency at a hospital or clinic for three to seven years, under the watchful eye of an experience physician, which will continue to build on the knowledge he has accumulated over the past 10 years. Completing the residency will allow him to begin his fellowship (specialty training) to become a heart surgeon. The fellowship can take a number of years, he would then be considered a heart surgeon.

    From the point, he began his journey to become a heart surgeon up to the point of him becoming one, he built over 20 years of working knowledge. For him to continue to practice medicine and maintain his status as a heart surgeon, he must continue his training and build on his 20+ years of knowledge until the day he retires. With no doubt, new procedures will come out, new technology will be introduced, and new techniques will become the standard practice in heart surgery. He must master and put the new knowledge to work, if he plans on continuing his practicing medicine as a heart surgeon.

Rich Men and Women understand the impact of mastering new knowledge and putting it to work. They understand to maintain their *True Riches* and obtain new Riches they must continue growing their knowledge and putting it work. They see knowledge as a life long journey, not a 100-meter sprint.

Working Knowledge

Keystones of the Pillar

1. Working Knowledge is putting the knowledge you've accumulated to work, in order to obtain your *Riches*.

2. Working Knowledge exercises intelligence and uses imagination.

3. Knowledge comes in many different forms. Do not discount where is comes from by its source. Investigate new knowledge before disregarding it.

4. Knowledge is a life long journey, not a 100 meter sprint.

Pillar VI - The Cohorts

"It's better to hang out with people better than you. Pick out associates whose behavior is better than yours and you'll drift in that direction"

Warren Buffet –

The Cohorts

The **Sixth Pillar** of Rich Man in Training is their **Cohorts.**

In ancient times, a *Cohort* was a military unit that represented one tenth of a legion in the Roman Army. Each *Cohort* was a tactical unit that had a specific assignment, which they carried out to protect the empire. One *Cohort* may have been responsible for civil order in the cities. Another *Cohort* may have been the Equites (cavalry), who were highly trained soldiers used to combat the enemy in war. These *Cohorts* proved to be so effective, they helped establish Rome as one of the strongest and most gifted empires known to man, successfully protecting the Roman Empire for nearly 1400 years.

Cohorts of a Rich Man

Rich Men have a legion of *Cohorts* who assist them in obtaining and protecting their *True Riches*, just as the Romans had Cohorts to protect their empire. These *Cohorts* are companions, mentors, students, fellows, and brain trust; whom all have a specific assignment, just as the Cohorts of Rome. Rich Men depend on these *Cohorts* to help build their empires. Establishing weak and ineffective *Cohorts*, results in failing to obtain *True Riches*. Building strong and effective *Cohorts,* results in obtaining and maintaining *True Riches*.

There is a minimum of five *Cohorts* you should acquire as a Rich Man in Training. These *Cohorts* are: The

Companion Cohort, The Upstream Cohort, The Down Stream Cohort, The Fellow Cohort, and The Counsel Cohort. Each one is instrumental to a Rich Man's cause, and serves a specific purpose to help him obtain and protect his *Riches*.

The Companion Cohort

The Companion Cohort is the most intimate group of individuals in a Rich Man's life. This may be his spouse, girlfriend, children, family, or friend. Normally, whoever is in the trusted inner circle.

The reason I began with this *Cohort*, is because it's the most important *Cohort* of the five. The Companion Cohort is the corner stone that builds a Rich Man's foundation. These individuals are those who feed the basic emotional needs (security, acceptance, love, sexual desires, or companionship). These individuals will have the deepest influence and greatest impact on you, good or bad. Therefore, you must be very selective in who you allow into this *Cohort*, as they can either tear you down or build you up. I've personally seen this go both ways.

In 1999, I met a young man that was in jail for attempted murder. Prior to him going to jail, he had an exemplary life. One that most of us would be proud to have. He had a beautiful wife, luxury home, foreign cars, great income, and a very bright future. Unfortunately, tragedy struck and he was stripped of his freedom, due to being betrayed by those in his Companion Cohort.

One day, he began to have suspicions that his wife was having an affair, due to her decrease of intimacy. He decided to confront her about his suspicions, when their level of intimacy had all but stopped. When he confronted her, she broke down in tears and told him that his close friend raped her, while he was a way on a business trip.

He became so infuriated. He loaded his handgun, drove to his friend's apartment, and shot him. Shortly after the shooting, he was arrested and charged with attempted murder.

Regardless of the consequence, he believed he did the noble thing. As he sat in jail, his wife broke the news to his lawyer, that she would not testify in court. She had been having an affair with his friend and was never raped.

There are millions of stories like this, in which a man or woman was on their road to *Riches*, but failed to obtain them, because someone in their Companion Cohort was cancerous. Although their story may not be as grim as the man I met in jail, the result is the same. One of their Companion Cohort became a distraction, causing conflict, displacement, deception, abandonment, worries, and/or concerns.

We should not be naive in thinking, "This would never happen to me!" As I previously stated, your Companion Cohort feeds your basic emotional needs. We tend to overlook the fact that an individual is cancerous, when they are fulfilling an emotional need. Consequently, we allow them to remain in their *Cohort* position, although they have proven to be menacing to us.

A True Rich Man clearly understands how much of an effect each person, within his Companion Cohort, can have on their ability to obtain their *True Riches*. Therefore, they'll selectively choose who will be in this *cohort*, and protect themselves by selecting people who'll always have their best interest at heart. They will purposely avoid a yes man, a leach, or negative Nate and Nancy, as a necessary strategy to obtaining their *True Riches*.

Key attributes on building a Companion Cohort that will help you build your *True Riches*.

1. Typically, the closest to us is our girlfriend, wife, or significant other. You must be very selective in whom you allow into this position. They are going to be your number one fan and catalyst in helping you obtain your *True Riches*. If you can't both contribute to one another in seeking your *True Riches*, then they are not the right person.

2. Those in your Companion Cohort should stimulate a mutual passion for success, love, and desire. If they do not share theses mutual passions, then you should

quickly work on finding out if there is a disconnect, and determine what is the causing factor. If you are not able to resolve the disconnect, cut your losses and move on. This is not to sound harsh, but you'll burn a lot of time and energy trying to fix something that may not be in either persons best interest.

3. Know what your companions desire most. If it's something that violates the natural laws of life, you must remove this person from your Companion Cohort. They will only bring you harm.

4. Attitude is infectious. If an individual in your Companion Cohort has a poor attitude or lack virtue in their character, then they should not be in your *Cohort*. Attitude is the toughest attribute to manage. In most circumstances, it is those closest to us that lack virtue and have a poor attitude. It is commonly a parent, best friend, spouse, or child. The closer the person is to you, the more of a distraction they will be. I too, have had to cut ties with the closest people to me. I love them, and will support them however I can, but I will not allow them in my Companion Cohort. They would inevitably become an obstruction, preventing me from focusing on obtaining my *True Riches*.

5. Your Companion Cohort should be individuals who are open and honest with you. These are individuals who spend the most time with you, and know you best. They should be able to help you see your faults and improve upon them, continuously. They should not just be *yes men*!

"Employ your time in improving yourself by other men's writings, so that you shall gain easily what others have labored hard for."

Socrates–

The Upstream Cohort

The Upstream Cohort represents your mentor group. I reference them as the Upstream Cohort, because they are the individuals who pass down their knowledge and guidance to help you obtain your *True Riches*. They are your *Nile River*, which will forever flow with knowledge, directly guiding you in obtaining your *True Riches*. Every Rich Man or Woman has a group of mentors that help them visualize what they can't see, give comprehension to what is not understood, and clarity to what they can't hear.

These mentors could be with them for a life time, or for a season. It is the job of a Rich Man in Training, to find their Upstream and listen without reservation.

The Cohorts

As a student of Drucker School of Management in 2016, I had the rare pleasure to meet Jim Hunt, retired CFO of Walt Disney Parks and Resorts, Peter Bavasi, former GM of Cleveland Indians, and John Bachmann, retired Managing Director of Edward Jones. Each of these men were influenced or personally mentored by Peter Drucker, the father of modern business management.

In the case of Peter Bavasi, he understood the true value of mentorship, and attributes his success to his mentors. His first mentor was his father, Buzzie Bavasi, an Executive in Major-League Baseball and a Hall of Famer. Buzzie Bavasi groomed Peter to become a professional baseball executive. Shortly after Buzzie Bavasi took the position as the first President of the San Diego Padres Baseball organization, Peter Bavasi was promoted as the Padres General Manager.

In 1973, Peter Bavasi gained a new mentor in the great Ray Kroc, owner of McDonald's fast food restaurants. In 1973 Ray Kroc purchased a majority share in the San Diego Padres. He took Peter under his arm, mentoring him in business and his personal life for years to come. Peter looked upon Ray Kroc as a second father.

In 1984, Peter Bavasi, headed to Cleveland, as the new President of the Cleveland Indians. When Peter took the position with the Cleveland Indians, they had one of the worst winning records in baseball. His new job was to change the entire organization from the inside out, and build a winning culture.

While he was sitting in his new office in Cleveland, trying to figure out how to build a winning culture in the Indians organization, he read an article written by Peter Drucker on management. He thought to himself, "I need to talk to this man, to help me figure out how to change the culture of this ball club."

So, Peter Bavasi, called the magazine publisher and asked if they could give him Peter Drucker's contact number. The man at the magazine laughed and told him Peter Drucker wouldn't help a baseball team; however, he gave him Drucker's home number.

When Bavasi reached Peter Drucker, he explained his situation and asked for his help. Peter Drucker agreed, and by the 1986 baseball season, Peter Bavasi built a winning culture, with the mentorship of Peter Drucker. In fact, this was their first winning season since the 1950s.

Now to think, Peter Bavasi had been groomed as an Executive for over 20 years. He was first mentored by his father, one of the only 2 men in American Baseball to become a Hall of Famer as an Executive, and then mentored by Ray Kroc, who bought and expanded McDonald's to become the largest fast food restaurants in the world. You could say he was mentored by the best, and gained all the experience, knowledge, and understanding on how to successfully run a baseball organization. So, why would Peter Bavasi seek out a new mentor in Peter Drucker?

Perter Bavasi understood the very principle of maintaining an Upstream Cohort. No matter how successful he became, he continued to seek the guidance, knowledge, and expertise of those who came before him. He started with his father, then Ray Kroc, and finally Peter Drucker.

Under all consideration, if a man as successful as Peter Bavasi maintained an Upstream Cohort, why should we believe that we can obtain our *True Riches* without such a *Cohort*? All Rich Men and Women have an Upstream Cohort, and holds them more valuable than gold.

Key attributes on building a Companion Cohort that will help you build your *True Riches*.

1. Find a mentor for each of your *Riches*. If one of your *Riches* is spirituality, then find a spiritual parent. If it's business, then find a successful business person. If it's to be a good parent, then connect with person who has proven to be a great parent.

2. Your mentor should know your *True Riches*. Be very transparent with them. The more open and honest you are with your mentor, the better they can help you.

3. You should have an open line to your mentor for questions, utilizing all resources: email, text, phone, visits, or instant messaging. You should be able to reach out to them at any time.

4. Schedule a standing appointment to meet with your mentor, periodically discussing your successes and failures. Give them the opportunity to advise you through the stumbling blocks, as well as the victories.

5. Contribute to your mentor. One of the biggest mistake I've seen made, is people do not look for ways to help their mentor. They are investing time into you, you must be willing to invest time into them.

"The best way a mentor can prepare another leader is to expose him or her to other great people."

John C. Maxwell–

The Downstream Cohort

A Rich Man in Training shall not obtain his *Riches,* if he is not willing to help others obtain theirs – It's just that simple. What you put into the world, is what you'll get back. This can be referred to as, **Knowledge Transfer**.

The more knowledge you transfer out, the more you'll receive. Therefore, all Rich Men will build a Downstream Cohort of individuals they'll personally mentor. I reference this *Cohort* as the Downstream Cohort, because you're pouring your knowledge into others. You're enrichening the lives of others, by sharing your knowledge.

Just about every great man or woman, you have ever heard about, has had a *Cohort* of people they've personally mentored. They provide others with specialized knowledge, needed to carry out missions. The Downstream Cohort is the reason I wrote this book. I could only reach out to so many people as one person; however, this book will allow me to reach out to the world, sharing my knowledge, and the knowledge of others, to those who would not be able to gain it otherwise.

I understand what it is like to want more, but don't have the knowledge or understanding on how to obtain your *Riches.* I know what it feels like, to feel less of a person, because of not having the specialized knowledge others may have; however, I've been blessed to have received a higher education. I've been blessed to meet Rich Men and Women of different walks of life. I've had the opportunity to learn from leaders in business, philosophy, religion, finances, and spirituality. It's now my personal responsibility to transfer this knowledge and mentor those who have yet to receive this opportunity.

When you openly mentor others, you're cultivating virtuous Companion Cohorts, building Upstream Cohorts that will pass down your knowledge and the knowledge of those who mentored you, create a Fellowship Cohorts, and you'll develop future Brain Trusts. Everything around you will flourish, because you are willing to mentor individuals who will build their future *cohorts*.

When I think of the Downstream Cohort, I think of Joel Osteen. He speaks of how his father, John Osteen, poured a fountain of knowledge into him, which paved the way for Joel to build the Lakewood Church into a beacon of light for the world. His father's mentorship empowered a young man to take over a church and elevate it to a level that allows his ministry to touch the lives of thousands, if not millions, today. Today, Joel Osteen mentors his *Cohort* to carry on the works of inspiration and hope. This is the power of the Downstream Cohort. It's a necessary component to carry on your mission in life.

The Cohorts

Key attributes on building a Downstream Cohort that will help you build your *True Riches*.

1. We all have something we are good at, such as cooking, business, art, or math. Your area of expertise is considered, specialized knowledge. Use this specialized knowledge to teach another person.

2. Give a set amount of time, a week or month, to mentor different individuals.

3. Everyone should mentor at least one person. Consider those who are in your daily environments: work, your community, or school.

4. Listen more than you speak, when you are mentoring someone. Allow them to get their thoughts and ideas out. Allow them to explore their own thoughts and ideas. Then share with them your knowledge and experiences.

> "Search well and be wise, nor believe that self-willed pride will ever be better than good counsel."
> Aeschylus –

The Counsel Cohort

Every Rich Man maintains a cabinet of individuals called the Counsel Cohort. This cabinet serves as their counsel, advising on all important matters. The more *Riches* and power one obtains, the greater this *Cohort* becomes.

Throughout history, emperors, kings, and presidents have held a cabinet who advised them on all matters, varying from war to public policy. With ever election of the United States presidency, the first order of business is to build their cabinet of individuals who will acts as their counsel. It's these individuals who guide the President by advising the best course of action to take in each situation. In the book *Think and Grow Rich*, by Napoleon Hill, this *Cohort* would be considered your **Mastermind Group**.

Each person in this *Cohort*, would have specialized knowledge in an area such as finances, law, spirituality, family, marriage, etc., which will help you make educated decisions.

Rich Men and Women understand, it's not logical for them to know everything. It's for them to know how to use the intelligence of others to help them obtain their *True Riches*. They are not too proud to build a phone book full of

The Cohorts

advisers, who will help them make important decisions. This is both effective and efficient. Many of us have heard the saying, "Work smarter, not harder." The use of the Counsel Cohort is one interpretation of this saying.

Rich Men look to cut their learning curve. They look to engage the brightest minds, in any given field, to help obtain their *Riches*. They don't exhaust their time trying to figure something out, when they have a resource of individuals to go to for advice.

A few years ago, I emailed an investor to discuss an idea of purchasing a technology company. He responded to my request with an agreement to set up a meeting to discuss the details, and a week later I was invited to meet at his office. When I arrived at his office, his assistant ushered me into a small office, where a man introduced himself to me as the investor's adviser. He explained his position of reviewing each investment opportunity, prior to the investor taking any interest in the concept or idea. If the advisor believed the opportunity made sense, he then presented the opportunity to a small committee of advisors to determine if they want to further explore the idea. If the group of advisers felt it was worth further exploring, they then presented the idea to the investor.

This process came as a surprise to me, because I had personally known the investor for over a year and never heard of his advisers. However, understanding this process, it is clear to me why many of his investments did well. He maintained a Counsel Cohort, which reviewed each opportunity, prior to investing his money. Every person in his *Cohort* had specific knowledge that helped him make educated decisions. He would not move forward on an opportunity, unless they gave him a nod of approval. If they did not give him the nod of approval, he simply walked away from the deal.

Each Rich Man will turn to his trusted advisers to make an important decision. A Rich Man is not so full of pride, that he chooses not to seek the advice of his counsel. He's smart enough to know he must use the intelligence of the experts to make a wise decision.

Key attributes on building a Counsel Cohort that will help you build your *True Riches*.

1. Build a phone book full of experts in various fields such as finance, insurance, law, business, spirituality, etc.

2. Build a relationship with individuals with specialized knowledge that you believe can help you obtain your *True Riches*.

3. Don't be fearful to ask those with specialized knowledge to help you with an important decision. Most of them will be flattered and happy to help.

"The TED Fellowship exposed me to a set of youngsters who had wilder ideas than I did - and almost all of them were pursuing their wild and crazy ideas without fear of failure."
Shaffi Mather -

The Fellow Cohort

Although a professional athlete may have a wife (Companion Cohort), coaches (Upstream Cohort), brother (downstream Cohort), and agent (Counsel Cohort), none of them will know what it feels like to be a professional athlete, unless they themselves were one. It's a distinct experience and unique perspective. No matter how well the professional athlete explains their experience to another person, that other person will never fully understand what it takes to be a professional athlete. This holds true in all areas of life. If you were a doctor, you could not ask your wife to answer a question on an advance medical procedure, if she were not a doctor herself. You would have to consult with a fellow doctor.

The Fellow Cohort is our peers in a profession or group. They are the people who can relate to us the best, because they share a common knowledge, speak the same language, and have the same unique perspective on challenges and success. There are many groups of people paying thousands of dollars a year to be a part of a Fellow Cohort. They understand the value they receive from being amongst their peers, learning and sharing ideas.

For example, there is an international organization, known as Vistage International, that is a Fellow Cohort for CEOs, Business Owners, and Executives. Vistage is a member only organization, where each member must pay over $10,000 a year to participate. Once a person is accepted as a Vistage member, they are placed into a selected group of peers. These individuals will meet at least once a month to share their experiences, ideas, and knowledge to help each other improve their abilities and skills as an organization leader. What makes this organization such a success, is that they are building Fellow Cohorts that learn from one another. In this case, most of their members are CEOs who share a unique perspective, of running a business or organization.

The Fellow Cohort is a very common practice in the business and leadership world. Executive and other leaders join a *Cohort* to help them develop their skills and abilities. Rich Men and Women are familiar with this concept. Therefore, they start or join Fellow Cohorts to helps them develop their knowledge and abilities. This is one of the best kept secrets that Rich Men and Women use time and time again to obtain their *True Riches*.

Key attributes on building a Fellow Cohort that will help you build your *True Riches*.

1. Start or join a peer group that shares the same type of understanding, ideas, knowledge, and concepts that you possess.

2. Find a fellow for each of your *Riches*. Someone, you can grow with and exchange ideas with. Your Fellow Cohort does not have to be limited to one area of life.

3. Your Fellow Cohort should encourage you to improve in all areas of life. They should help you stay on track and inspire you. Remember, they are your peers who can sharpen your abilities. They can offer you specialized insight that you both share.

Keystones of the Pillar

1. Your Companion Cohort is the corner stone *Cohort*. Your ability to obtain *Riches* will hinge on you building a strong and encouraging Companion Cohort.

2. Your Upstream Cohort will pour their knowledge into you, giving you the understanding and know how to obtain your *True Riches*.

3. Your Downstream Cohort will grow your *Riches* as you develop other individuals. By pouring the knowledge you gained into them, a ripple effect is created and an influence is released, encouraging others to create their own *Cohort*.

4. Your Counsel Cohort is the *Cohort* you will use to make wise decisions. This *Cohort* will keep you from making erroneous decisions that could block you or slow down your ability to obtain your *True Riches*.

5. Your Fellow Cohort will have the special insight to help you obtain your *True Riches*. Those in this *Cohort* have experienced the success and failures in a common area, such as business.

Pillar VII – Resourceful Fear

"If you want to conquer fear, don't sit home and think about it. Go out and get busy"

Dale Carnegie–

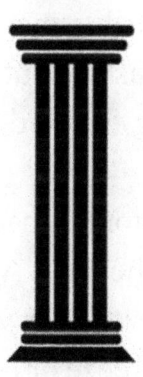

Resourceful Fear

The **Seventh Pillar** of a Rich Man in Training is **Resourceful Fear.** Without question, fear exist. It's a natural psychological and physical reaction that is meant to protect us from circumstances that we perceive as dangerous. It's our primal defense system which has protected humans for millions of years. Unfortunately, through learned behavior we began to use fear in unnatural ways, to protect us from things that don't exist. What do I mean by this? How many times have you worried about something that has not happened or does not happen? You're sitting paralyzed in fear, anticipating that this something will come to pass and it never does. Think of the time you wasted, but more importantly how it stopped you from moving forward while you pondered upon it.

This learned behavior has become so powerful, that we subconsciously do it all the time. We ponder upon fear after fear, never moving forward. Fear was never meant to makes us afraid and cause us to freeze or run. It was meant to benefit us. Rich Men understand this very essence and practice using fear as a resource to benefit them to obtain their *True Riches*. To understand how they do this you must first understand how fear works at the physiological and physical layers.

How Fear Works

Say for example you hear something crash through your bedroom window. The nerves in your ears will send a signal to your *Thalamus,* which is the relay station in the center of your brain. Your *Thalamus* will relay the signals to your *Amygdala,* and activate key neurotransmitters to send signals to your *Periaqueductal Gray* and *Hypothalamus,* which are both responsible to how you react when you perceive a danger.

When the neurotransmitters rush to your *Periaqueductal Gray*, it activates the primal area of your brain, causing you to either freeze or jump. In most cases you'll freeze, look, and listen, just like a deer does when they hear something in the woods as they are drinking from the stream. The main reason we freeze is because it's an instinct that helps us avoid a predator from detecting us through movement, which was very important for our ancestors' survival.

Then the second area of your brain the neurotransmitters will rush to is *Hypothalamus*. This area is responsible for your autonomic nervous system, which causes your heart rate to increase, blood pressure to rise, and respiratory rate to change by releasing adrenaline from our adrenal glands into regions of your body. It's this area that determines if you fight or flight.

Resourceful Fear

When you get to the point of fight or flight, it's a conscious decision to determine if the threat to you or someone else is great enough to mobilize by fighting for fleeing. Once this decision is made you'll follow through until the danger is no longer there.

The most interesting thing about the entire process is, it's all perception. You can use fear to obtain your *riches* by using it as it was intended to protect you, or it can become a detriment to you and tear you down.

"Thoughts are mental energy; they're the currency that you have to attract what you desire. Learn to stop spending that currency on thoughts you don't want."

Wayne Dyer-

Fear as a Resource

What if I walked up to you and told you that in the next 4 seconds a speeding car was going to jump the curb and land right in the spot that you are standing, and the only way you could avoid being hit is by jumping into the street? Would you? I believe you would. Why? Because your perception that running into the street was less harmful to you than standing on the curb at that moment, which is a benefit to you.

This is how Rich Men operate. They develop a system to use fear as a resource to benefit themselves. If they feel that something is a threat to obtaining their *Riches*, that threat now becomes greater than any fear, worry, or concern they may have at that time. Therefore, Rich Men will use the fear of that threat to activate their instinct of survival, and conquer it. While most of us will allow our doubts, fears, and worries to consume our mind, causing us to freeze, Rich Men have activated the *Hypothalamus* part of their brain, starting the process to use fear as a resource and benefit to their protection. They harness their fear and use it to generate the strength, vision, and the courage needed to obtain their *Riches*.

Rich Men turn their fear into fire. They turn their fear into *Zeal*. *Zeal* is an energy fueled by the source of fear. The more fear a Rich Man has, the more *Zeal* he produces. Fear is a fuel that combusts within his very soul, which ignites him to become mobile, rather than becoming paralyzed.

My First Use of Fear as a Resource

I began using my fear as a resource while I was in prison. In my first three years of incarceration, I was heavily involved with prison gangs. I was associated with a certain group that was known for a high level of violence and a wide

Resourceful Fear

range of mischief. Once you joined the gang, you had to participate in acts that could easily extend your prison stay, into a life sentence.

If anyone desired to disconnect from the gang it was only two ways to do this. You could either go into protective custody or by death. If you went into protective custody, you had to debrief (snitch) to the authorities, giving information on how your gang operates, within and outside the prison. This would put a mark on you and your family within their reach. Therefore, the perception was very clear. Once you join the gang, you signed the contract in blood.

During the beginning of my third year in prison, I had a phone conversation with my mother-in-law. She raised her concerns about my daughter's future and wellbeing, without possibly having a father. This struck me deeply, because of all the young women I have personally known, who took the dark path in life due to not having a father to guide and protect them.

My thoughts began to haunt me. I couldn't have my daughter growing up without her father. I could not have my daughter latching onto some young man, who may take advantage of her. However, the activities I was assigned to within my gang, would almost guarantee I would receive an extended prison sentence, and possibly remain in that place for life.

The fear that began to stir in my mind, led me to contemplate my choices. Do I walk away from the gang, or do I continue taking risks that would keep me in prison? Over the course of a few months, my concerns for my daughter and girlfriend built into an unease from within. This unease was grow greater than the fear and anxiety of what would happen if I walked away from my gang. It was at this point, I had to choose would I let this fear paralyze me or become my zeal and mobilize me to act. I decided it was going to become my zeal.

My girlfriend and daughter were all I had of value, my *True Riches*. The fear of losing them was the fuel needed to move me in the right direction. It provided me the courage necessary to walk away from my gang, regardless of the serious nature and threat this decision would have on my life. My disassociation was probably one the most dangerous types, because I chose not to go into protective custody, but to face any consequences by disassociating with my gang even if that meant death. I simply decided to tell my gang that I was out and no longer wanted to be associated with them.

Needless to say, my disassociation did not go over very well and created a very hostile situation for me; however, my fear of losing my daughter was greater than any fear you could imagine – Even death! My fear of losing my daughter motivated me to mobilize. I could not sit in fear, and stay the same person, and envision the reality of not coming through for her.

the course of my last 18 months in prison, was one of the scariest times in my life. I did not know if or when they were going to hold true to their threats. I had already been in several altercations and prayed that I would survive until my release. Well, I did survive, and the fear of losing my daughter greatly became my benefit.

More importantly, I'm proud to say my daughter is a great student preparing to graduate from one of the best private schools in my area. She was not exposed to the cruelties of the world, as I know many other young ladies have been.

The fear of losing my family did more than just mobilize me to disassociate from my gang and get out of prison. I used it as a resource to obtain a great college education, build my income, and cultivate a wonderful life for my family. My fear became my fuel, the zeal to mobilize me. It continues to do so as I build businesses and help others.

"We have been brainwashed into craving a diet that is killing us. What we believe tastes good is generally what we have been socially conditioned to enjoy."

Jane Velez-Mitchell -

Brainwashed by Fear

Fear allows us to become brainwashed and accept what is not good for us. You must un-wash your brain and use fear as your resource to not accept what is bad for you.

A few years ago, I was counseling a young woman on career development. She had told me ever reason why she couldn't succeed in life. Every reason she gave me was a reason of fear. She was blinded by her fear. She worried about her husband leaving her if she went back to college. She worried about not being smart enough to take a promotion. She didn't like to go out, because she was fearful of spending too much money.

Everything she mentioned had some type of fear associated with it. So, I asked her, "Aren't you fearful that you'll end up 70 years old asking what happened to my life? Aren't you fearful of what type of example you are setting for your daughter to see her mother frozen by her fears?"

I could tell that she had not thought much about it. She became brainwashed by her fears. As she delayed acting on her desires, her fears became her reality.

She lived with this mindset for so long, she began to invent fears. She worried about things she had no control over, nor would have any real effect on her ability to obtain *True Riches*. She developed a pre-condition to believe she was unworthy of obtaining her *True Riches*. Because of her fears, she was cheated out of life.

Resourceful Fear

Rich Men and Women, will never allow their fears to be the factor that stops them. When most of us would slam on the brake pedal in an uncertain situation. Rich Men press on the gas and accelerate!

Turn Fears into Action

As a final exercise in this book, I would like you to do the following:

1. Fold a paper into three columns.
2. In the first column write down all your fears.
3. In the second column, I want you to write out what your fears are stopping you from accomplishing.
4. In the third column, I want you to write down what you are losing by not accomplishing the things that are being stopped by your fears.
5. I want you to look at each fear and ask yourself,

    "Is my fear of not obtaining what's in column three more than the fear that's stopping me from obtaining it?"

This is how you'll begin breaking through each of the fears that has been a detriment to your successes in life and obtaining your *True Riches*.

As a free resource you can download the **"Rich Man in Training – Turn Your Fear in Resources – Worksheet'** at **richmanintraining.com** to complete this exercise.

Keystones of the Pillar

1. Use fear to mobilize you, not paralyze you.

2. Your desires, should out weight your thoughts of fear.

3. How you perceive fear, is how you'll be able to use it as a resource.

4. We've been brainwashed by our fears; however, you have the power to un wash your brain.

In Conclusion

Understand being a **Rich Man in Training**, is not for a season. It's a life long journey. As we obtain our *Riches*, we'll continue to expand and look for more as we grow as individuals. What may be your *Riches* today, may not be your *Riches* tomorrow. You can also view this as, the *Riches* you obtain today, is part of your path to obtaining other *Riches* in life.

What constitutes *True Riches*, are the desires that will enrichen your life and the lives of others. The more you enrichen the lives of others, the more likely you'll obtain your *True Riches*. What you put into the universe is what you'll get back.

These 7 Pillars are just the beginning of becoming a True Rich Man. As you obtain your *True Riches* through the practicing of theses 7 Pillars, you'll find your quality of life increasing. You will become filled with abundance in love, business, finance, friendship, family, spirituality, and all other areas of your life. This is what happened to me.

Every day I wake up with excitement knowing what my *True Riches* are, and that I'm on the road to obtain them.

I pray that you too, feel and see the abundance that life has to offer. The profusions that come with obtaining your *True Riches* brings you true happiness, and the commitment you make to becoming a **Rich Man in Training** ensures you'll obtain your Riches!

BIOs

- In alphabetical order by first name-

Aeschylu - (525/524 – c. 456/455 BC) was an ancient Greek tragedian. He is often described as the father of tragedy. Academics' knowledge of the genre begins with his work, and understanding of earlier tragedies is largely based on inferences from his surviving plays. According to Aristotle, he expanded the number of characters in theater allowing conflict among them; characters previously had interacted only with the chorus.

Albert Einstein – (14 March 1879 – 18 April 1955) was a German-born theoretical physicist. He developed the general theory of relativity, one of the two pillars of modern physics (alongside quantum mechanics).Einstein's work is also known for its influence on the philosophy of science.[6][7] Einstein is best known in popular culture for his mass–energy equivalence formula $E = mc^2$ (which has been dubbed "the world's most famous equation").He received the 1921 Nobel Prize in Physics "for his services to Theoretical Physics, and especially for his discovery of the law of the photoelectric effect a pivotal step in the evolution of quantum theory

Arnold Bennett - (27 May 1867 – 27 March 1931) was an English writer. He is nowadays best known as a novelist, but he also worked in other fields such as the theatre, journalism, propaganda and film.

Charles Morgan - (22 January 1894 – 6 February 1958) was an English-born playwright and novelist of English and Welsh parentage. The main themes of his work were, as he himself put it, "Art, Love, and Death",[1] and the relation between them. Themes of individual novels range from the paradoxes of freedom (*The Voyage, The River Line*), through passionate love seen from within (*Portrait in a Mirror*) and without (*A Breeze of Morning*), to the conflict of good and evil (*The Judge's Story*) and the enchanted boundary of death (*Sparkenbroke*). He was the husband of Welsh novelist Hilda Vaughan.

Dale Carnegie - (November 24, 1888 – November 1, 1955) was an American writer and lecturer and the developer of famous courses in self-improvement, salesmanship, corporate training, public speaking, and interpersonal skills. Born into poverty on a farm in Missouri, he was the author of *How to Win Friends and Influence People* (1936), a bestseller that remains popular today. He also wrote *How to Stop Worrying and Start Living* (1948), *Lincoln the Unknown* (1932), and several other book.

Herbert Spencer - (27 April 1820 – 8 December 1903) was an English philosopher, biologist, anthropologist, sociologist, and prominent classical liberal political theorist or the Victorian ear. Spencer developed an all-embracing conception of evolution as the progressive development of the physical world, biological organisms, the human mind, and human culture and societies. As a polymath, he contributed to a wide range of subjects, including ethics, religion, anthropology, economics, political theory, philosophy, literature, astronomy, biology, sociology, and psychology.

Hilary Hinton "Zig" Ziglar– (November 6, 1926 – November 28, 2012) was an American author, salesman, and motivational speaker.

Jane Velez-Mitchell – is a television journalist and author. For six years she hosted her own show on HLN, *Jane Velez-Mitchell* (formerly known as *Issues with Jane Velez-Mitchell*) replacing Glenn Beck, who moved to Fox News Channel. She is often seen commenting on high-profile cases for CNN, TruTV, E! and other national cable TV shows. Velez-Mitchell frequently guest hosts for Nancy Grace on her Headline News show. Velez-Mitchell reported for the nationally syndicated show *Celebrity Justice*.

John C. Maxwell - (born 1947) is an American author, speaker, and pastor who has written many books, primarily focusing on leadership. Titles include *The 21 Irrefutable Laws of Leadership* and *The 21 Indispensable Qualities of a Leader*. His books have sold millions of copies, with some on the New York Times Best Seller List.

Kristin Armstrong – (born August 11, 1973) is a professional road bicycle racer and three-time Olympic gold medalist, the winner of the women's individual time trial in 2008, 2012 and 2016. Before temporarily retiring to start a family in 2009, she rode for Cervélo TestTeam in women's elite professional events on the National Racing Calendar (NRC) and UCI Women's World Cup. She announced a return to competitive cycling beginning in the 2011 season, competing for Peanut Butter & Co. TWENTY12 at the Redlands Classic.

Martin Luther King, Jr. - (January 15, 1929 – April 4, 1968) was an American Baptist minister and activist who was a leader in the Civil Rights Movement. He is best known for his role in the advancement of civil rights using nonviolent civil disobedience based on his Christian beliefs.

Napoleon Hill – (born **Oliver Napoleon Hill**; October 26, 1883 – November 8, 1970) was an American self-help author inspired by the New Thought movement. He is well known for his book *Think and Grow Rich* (1937) which has sold 20 million copies. Hill's works insisted that fervid expectations are essential to improving one's life. Most of his books were promoted as expounding principles to achieve "success."

Norman Vincent Peale – (May 31, 1898 – December 24, 1993) was an American minister and author known as a progenitor of positive thinking, which was typified in his popular book *The Power of Positive Thinking*.

Peter F. Drucker – (November 19, 1909 – November 11, 2005) was an Austrian-born American management consultant, educator, and author, whose writings contributed to the philosophical and practical foundations of the modern business corporation. He was also a leader in the development of management education, he invented the concept known as management by objectives and self-control, and he has been described as "the founder of modern management"

Saint Augustine – (13 November 354 – 28 August 430) was an early Christian theologian and philosopher whose writings influenced the development of Western Christianity and Western philosophy. He was the bishop of Hippo Regius (within modern-day Annaba, Algeria), located in Numidia (Roman province of Africa). Augustine is viewed as one of the most important Church Fathers in Western Christianity for his writings in the Patristic Era. Among his most important works are *The City of God* and *Confessions*.

Saint Augustine – (13 November 354 – 28 August 430) was an early Christian theologian and philosopher whose writings influenced the development of Western Christianity and Western philosophy. He was the bishop of Hippo Regius (within modern-day Annaba, Algeria), located in Numidia (Roman province of Africa). Augustine is viewed as one of the most important Church Fathers in Western Christianity for his writings in the Patristic Era. Among his most important works are *The City of God* and *Confessions*.

Samuel Smiles – (23 December 1812 – 16 April 1904), was a Scottish author and government reformer who campaigned on a Chartist platform. But he concluded that more progress would come from new attitudes than from new laws. His masterpiece, *Self-Help* (1859), promoted thrift and claimed that poverty was caused largely by irresponsible habits, while also attacking materialism and laissez-faire government. It has been called "the bible of mid-Victorian liberalism", and it raised Smiles to celebrity status almost overnight.

Shaffi Mather - (born February 6, 1970) is an Indian social entrepreneur, who served as the Economic Advisor to the Chief Minister, Oommen Chandy, of Kerala's Congress led, UDF Government. He also worked, for a short period, as an advisor to Rahul Gandhi He is a lawyer. Shaffi has also worked in the Real Estate sector, along with his brothers. In April 2010, he attended the Entrepreneur Summit which was held at Washington DC, at the invitation of US President Barack Obama. In his capacity as Economic Advisor, he was responsible for bringing the World Economic Forum community retreat, to be held in November 2013 to Kochi.

Socrates – (470/469 – 399 BC) was a classical Greek (Athenian) Philosopher credited as one of the founders of Western philosophy. He is an enigmatic figure known chiefly through the accounts of classical writers, especially the writings of his students Plato and Xenophon and the plays of his contemporary Aristophanes. Plato's dialogues are among the most comprehensive accounts of Socrates to survive from antiquity, though it is unclear the degree to which Socrates himself is "hidden behind his 'best disciple', Plato."

Steve Jobs – (February 24, 1955 – October 5, 2011) was an American businessman, inventor, and industrial designer. He was the co-founder, chairman, and chief executive officer (CEO) of Apple Inc.; CEO and majority shareholder of Pixar; a member of The Walt Disney Company's board of directors following its acquisition of Pixar; and founder, chairman, and CEO of NeXT. Jobs is widely recognized as a pioneer of the microcomputer revolution of the 1970s and 1980s, along with Apple co-founder Steve Wozniak.

Thomas Aquinas – Italian: *Tommaso d'Aquino*, lit. 'Thomas of Aquino'; 1225 – 7 March 1274), was an Italian Dominican friar, Catholic priest, and Doctor of the Church. He was an immensely influential philosopher, theologian, and jurist in the tradition of scholasticism, within which he is also known as the **Doctor Angelicus** and the **Doctor Communis**. The name *Aquinas* identifies his ancestral origins in the county of Aquino in present-day Lazio.

Walter Bagehot– (3 February 1826 – 24 March 1877) was a British journalist, businessman, and essayist, who wrote extensively about government, economics, and literature.

Warren Buffet - (born August 30, 1930) is an American investor, business magnate, and philanthropist. He is considered by some to be one of the most successful investors in the world, and as of February 2017, is the second wealthiest person in the world with a total net worth of $73.9 billion.

Wayne Dyer - (May 10, 1940 – August 29, 2015) was an American philosopher, self-help author, and motivational speaker. His first book, *Your Erroneous Zones* (1976), is one of the best-selling books of all time, with an estimated 35 million copies sold to date

*All Bios were supplied by Wikipedia

FREE RESOURCES

Visit our website www.richmanintraining.com *to get your FREE Worksheets, Planners, What's Your Time Worth Calculator, Monthly Riches Review and more.*

Time Study Worksheet

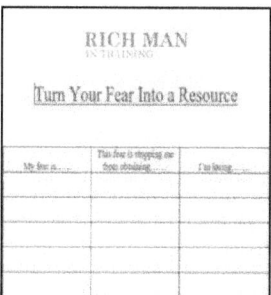

Turn Your Fear into a Resource - Worksheet

Riches, Goals, and Task Planner

Riches Tracker

What's Your Time Worth Calculator

Accountability Letter - Template

www.ingramcontent.com/pod-product-compliance
Lightning Source LLC
Chambersburg PA
CBHW071704040426
42446CB00011B/1905